Common Good Capitalism is a breath of fresh air blowing through stagnant thinking about income and wealth disparity and the failures of capitalist societies. Asesh Sarkar uses his own personal experiences to unblinkingly describe how the ordinary person has been losing ground to wealthy holders of capital for the last 45 years in the US and the UK, and how that undermines the social contract. But instead of looking for solutions in a fractured political world, he describes how the concept of 'co-ownership' – a plan to align corporate incentives with sustainable wealth distribution through customer share allocations – can change society and business in a positive way while maintaining all the growth benefits of the capitalist system. Sarkar's research demonstrates how companies can use co-ownership to increase loyalty, goodwill and share of wallet, and gain market insights through an activated customer/investor base. Customers will benefit from share ownership, regular dividends, financial literacy and a voice in corporate decisions as they become partners with their favoured brands. Business leaders should leap at the opportunity to do well and do good by helping their customers join the ownership society.

Todd H. Baker – senior fellow at the Richman Center for Business, Law and Public Policy at Columbia Business and Law Schools and managing principal at Broadmoor Consulting LLC

Asesh Sarkar tackles the stark inequalities in contemporary capitalism, illustrating how the rich get richer while the poor fall further behind. He presents a realistic and achievable win–win solution, offering a path to financial stability for millions in our society. Asesh's upbringing in Leicester, his role as a social entrepreneur with Salary Finance and his leadership at MyBnk, the UK's leading financial education charity, equip him with the expertise and credibility to present this transformative alternative.

Peter Heneghan – founder of The Future Communicator and former chief digital communicator to the UK government

Against a background of rising inequality, despair and despondency of millions who can't get ahead financially, this wonderful book sets out how capitalism can be reinvented to help deliver hope, power and wealth to the many, not just the few.

Jason Butler – columnist, *Financial Times* and personal finance expert.

COMMON GOOD CAPITALISM

A **NEW** ECONOMIC MODEL FOR GROWTH TO BENEFIT BUSINESS AND SOCIETY

Asesh Sarkar

Common Good Capitalism
ISBN 978-1-915483-55-3 (paperback)
ISBN 978-1-915483-57-7 (hardback)
ISBN 978-1-915483-56-0 (ebook)

Published in 2024 by Right Book Press

Contents

The big idea

Before we begin: Throughout this book, I'll be using the term 'common person' to represent the ordinary working person. This isn't intended to be derogatory. I chose 'common person' to tie in with the title of the book, *Common Good Capitalism*.

On both sides of the Atlantic, the common person is becoming increasingly impoverished. The latest UK government data shows that 14.4 million people are living in poverty (Francis-Devine 2024). This includes 4.2 million children – almost one in three. In the US, also based on the latest government data, 37.9 million Americans are living in poverty (Lee 2023). Millennials (born in the 1980s/90s) are the first generation in recent history to have less wealth than their parents at the same age (Luhby 2020).

There are many other statistics that tell the same story. For most people, however, statistics are not required: they feel it or see it every day. The impoverishment of the common person has implications for us all, whether we're rich, poor or somewhere in between. The million (well, trillion) dollar question is, what can be done about it?

The economic system of a country should lift society as a whole. In the UK and US – the focus of this book – that economic system is capitalism. Today, capitalism is no longer lifting society as a whole. It's broken. When a bank fails, to quote Ernest Hemingway, it fails 'gradually, then suddenly'. The same is happening to capitalism. After decades of 'gradual' decline, we're now in the 'suddenly' failing phase. To address the mass impoverishment of the common person, we must address the failings of capitalism in today's world.

After the Second World War, right up until the 1980s, capitalism delivered unprecedented levels of economic and social progress on both sides of the Atlantic. It became the overarching economic system, with varying levels of government intervention. During this period, there was consistent economic growth and rising 'real' wages (discounting for inflation) for the common person. There was, of course, inequality, which is a by-product of capitalism, but on the whole, society was on the rise. You can see this in Figure 1.

Since the 1980s, that dynamic has changed. As you can also see in the chart, economic growth continued to rise after the 1980s but average real wages for the common person have remained broadly flat in the decades since. This leads to a fundamental question: who has been benefiting from this economic growth? The answer is: shareholders. Economic growth has been driven by the growth of big companies, the beneficiaries of which are their owners (ie shareholders). And who are the shareholders? In the US, the wealthiest 10 per cent own 92 per cent of public company shares and the least wealthy 50 per cent own just 0.25 per cent (Dudley & Rouen 2021a). In the UK, the picture is slightly less extreme but the wealthiest 10 per cent still own 63 per cent of shares and the least wealthy 50 per cent own only 10 per cent (ONS 2021).

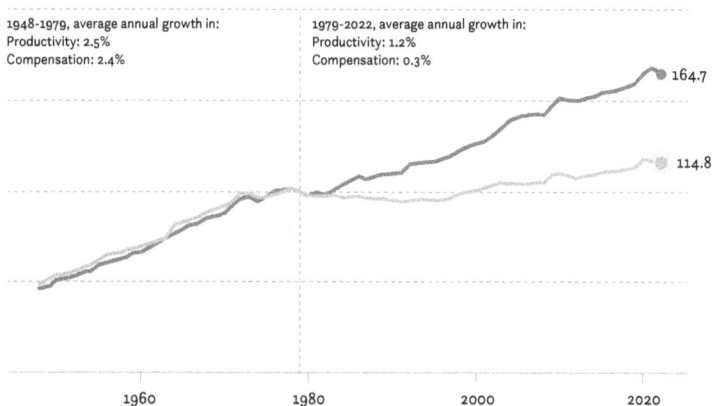

1948-1979, average annual growth in:
Productivity: 2.5%
Compensation: 2.4%

1979-2022, average annual growth in:
Productivity: 1.2%
Compensation: 0.3%

164.7

114.8

1960   1980   2000   2020

Figure 1: Productivity growth and hourly compensation growth, 1948–2021

Shareholders are typically those who are already wealthy and economic growth simply increases this further. Capitalism has led to a polarised society, split between the common people and shareholders. The common person lives off their wages, which have seen barely any growth since the 1980s. Shareholders live off their investments, which have seen continued growth, resulting in increased wealth accumulation.

There's an additional factor at play here that deepens this polarisation of society. We live in times where there are literally endless things to buy at the click of a button, with enormous marketing budgets enticing us to do so and no formal financial education in schools or later in life to teach good money habits. This has led to a popular culture of spending rather than saving or investing. And so, while real wages remain flat, wealth for most people is going backwards, as spending is prioritised above saving and investing.

I've been a common person as well as a shareholder – and I've experienced life as both relatively poor and relatively rich. In my experience, while money and wealth don't buy happiness, a lack of money creates stress and impacts all aspects of life. At the same time, when inequality keeps rising (the rich keep getting richer and the poor keep getting poorer), this naturally leads to social and political tensions. My fear, based on reading the economic data and studying similar times in history and human behaviour, is that the impoverishment of the common person and the resulting inequality are fast reaching breaking point. I believe this will lead to mass social unrest that will impact us all for generations to come.

This is where my big idea comes in: an innovation that ensures capitalism delivers for the common person as well as shareholders. The idea is called the customer co-ownership economy, or 'co-owned' for short. Co-owned is a new economic model in which big companies issue at least 10 per cent of their shares to their customers, rewarding customer loyalty and creating customer co-owners. In return, through increased loyalty and engagement, customer co-owners help to increase the value of those companies by more than the value of the shares issued to them. An almost universal truth for every company is that its long-term value is determined by how loyal and engaged its customers are, and customer co-ownership is a meaningful way in which to foster loyalty and engagement.

Throughout this book I shall use the term 'co-owned' to encompass the co-ownership concept; later I will also introduce Co-owned with a capital 'C', our research and technology organisation which will help businesses test and implement being co-owned.

The co-owned economic model creates a win for all, including for the common person, as across big companies almost everyone is a customer. Customers benefit directly from the value of shares they receive for their loyalty as they go about their day-to-day spending. But, just as importantly, this provides a way for the common person to connect with and learn about how shares in big companies work, and to use that financial education to help them save and invest for their future. Co-owned puts the common person on the same side as shareholders, bringing them closer together and enabling them to grow together for the benefit of all. It creates a society full of shareholders.

As an added benefit of co-owned and as big business shapes more of our society, having a more diverse shareholder base and input adds a much-needed level of democratic decision making in how these businesses are run. For example, an Amazon shareholder recently explained to me how they were able to vote and have their say on a range of topics, including an employee share incentive plan, gender and racial pay practices, DE&I (diversity, equity and inclusion) and warehouse working conditions.

Continuing the status quo is unlikely to be an option. History tells us that as wealth inequality intensifies, mass social unrest follows. If capitalism continues to fail to lift society as a whole, there are two likely paths ahead, just as in the 1920s and 1930s:

➡ Democracy is challenged as authoritarian leaders with extremist ideologies gain traction on the back of public anger and disillusionment.
➡ Democratic leaders have no choice but to redistribute wealth through interventionist government and growing taxes.

Neither is likely to be good for business, shareholders or society.

Today, co-owned is a concept. In this book, I will set out arguments and supporting data for why it's necessary, the benefits it can bring and how it can be implemented. It's aimed at inspiring executives and shareholders in big companies to think about their shareholder returns in the context of the realities of life for their customers. Arguably, they owe those customers a duty of care – and by making customers co-owners, this could benefit companies, customers and society as a whole: the classic win–win–win. My hope is that this book inspires a movement of companies to become customer co-owned for the common good.

2

My story and influences

Be the change you want to see happen.
– Arleen Lorrance (attributed to Gandhi)

This chapter tells a short version of my life story so far. Not because I'm a narcissist – in fact, the opposite is closer to the truth, as I'm a natural introvert – but because everyone is influenced by their life experiences, so I want to be upfront about mine. I'll start by managing your expectations and telling you what I'm not and what this book is not. I'm not an economist, historian or sociologist – all lenses through which capitalism can be viewed. And I don't have any alliances with a political party or ideology. This book is a business book, not a book about politics or academia. Of course, business operates within an economic system, which the government influences and academics study. But the primary purpose of this book is to set out a course of action that's good for business and necessary in my opinion for the economic and societal system in which it operates.

I'm a social entrepreneur, born to an immigrant working-class family. Through education, hard work and professional successes, I've moved into the shareholder class. I'm an example of social mobility and what capitalism can do when it works well. I've experienced and can empathise with the realities of life across different income and wealth levels. I believe that the problems with capitalism today are not (generally) due to bad actors but an economic system that needs to correct its course, which business leaders can and should lead on.

There are, of course, other areas that must be continually addressed to build a financially healthier society, such as education and job training programmes that improve access to opportunities for all. This book doesn't address these wider areas – not because they're unimportant but because without a way for the general population to benefit from economic growth, they're not sufficient to address the fundamental issues with capitalism today. To bring these fundamental issues to life, it's instructive to look at my life and professional experiences to see how they influenced me to create the co-owned model.

Childhood in inner-city Leicester (1981–1998)

I was born in inner-city Leicester (in the UK) in 1981, the second child to my first-generation Indian immigrant parents, Jharna and Bibhuti. My brother Bidesh is 12 years older than me and left for university when I was six, so much of my childhood was just me and my parents and then, when my dad passed away, just me and my mum.

In our working-class immigrant family, money was a constant challenge and point of contention during my childhood. However, this tension was compensated for with a lot of love. My parents' main aim was to prioritise education for me and my brother, as that was the biggest gift they could give us (and arguably the biggest gift any parent can give their child).

I learned two important money lessons during my childhood, which have influenced my thinking on co-owned. First, my mum and dad perfectly represented the two financial archetypes that most people fit into. It wasn't until later in life that I realised this, after a major research project at my last company (more on that later). My mum is what my researchers described as a 'planner'. A planner is someone who budgets carefully, who saves first and spends later. We didn't have much money growing up and I can remember my mum budgeting meticulously on pieces of paper. I recall her often saying that she couldn't wait for the day when we could do the weekly shop at Somerfield (a UK supermarket chain later bought by the Co-op) and not need to count the pennies to ensure we had enough. Despite this, in my mum's household budget, there was a line item for savings and investments. Investments required monthly payments and would typically take a few years to mature.

My dad was what my researchers described as a 'coper'. A coper is someone who doesn't spend much time budgeting, who spends first and saves later (with later rarely coming). I recall my dad repeatedly questioning my mum as to why she was putting money away into savings and investments when we barely had the money to live week to week. To be fair, it was a reasonable question, especially because these investments would take years to mature and we had so many pressing money challenges.

Sure enough, though, before we knew it, the years would pass, the investments would mature and they provided some easing of the pressure on the family finances. With the benefit of hindsight, we were always glad that my mum had put the money away.

In today's world, most people are copers like my late dad. We live in a culture where people spend first and save and invest later. There are fewer people like my mum, natural planners who budget carefully and minimise costs today to save and invest for the future. As a result, there's a huge savings and investments gap in the UK and US. In the UK, one in six adults have no savings and one in four have less than £100 (O'Brien 2024). In the US, nearly two in five Americans don't have the money to cover a $400 emergency expense (Federal Reserve System 2022). Many people with no savings or investments often put it down to insufficient income. I do wonder, however, whether the real issue is their natural money archetype, being a coper rather than a planner, and whether a planner in their shoes would find a way to save and invest, just like my mum did.

Linking this to co-owned. There's no, or very limited, financial education in schools (more on what I'm doing in that area later) and most people either:

➡ don't understand savings and investments
➡ or, even if they do, are still copers.

For the majority, the penny hasn't dropped on the benefits and indeed the necessity of being a planner and the importance of savings and investments in building future wealth. Through co-owned, consumers can earn share investments for free in companies they ordinarily spend money on or use, which would have the natural benefit of helping them learn about how investments work (including associated topics such as compound growth and passive income) without any special effort. For many, this could be the start of their savings and investments habit, which they can then build on. This has the potential to help a generation of copers learn about finances and take the first step to becoming planners and building wealth. Today, my mum is thankfully financially free. Money is no longer a constraint on her life and that's entirely down to her planner mentality and discipline.

The second money lesson from my childhood is how transformative it is to receive an unexpected windfall payment when living pay cheque to pay cheque and how much goodwill it creates. As is the case for many growing up today, there are many times when costs are higher than you expect but rarely a time when income is. But when your income is unexpectedly boosted, it's a cause for huge joy and relief.

When I was growing up, my parents banked with the Bradford & Bingley building society. As a mutual society, Bradford & Bingley was owned by its members, who were also its customers. These members held certain rights and benefits, such as having a say in the governance of the society. When a mutual society demutualises, it converts to being a stock-based company and is no longer owned by its members. As a result of this change, the members are compensated for the loss of their ownership rights and benefits. In the case of Bradford & Bingley, eligible members received cash payments. My parents received just over £1,000, which was a lot of money to us in those days. I clearly remember this windfall today, 25 or so years on, and remember Bradford & Bingley with much fondness for it.

Linking this to co-owned. As companies reward their customers with real shares that have real value (including a share in profits through dividends), I expect the level of goodwill for the many people living pay cheque to pay cheque will be huge – just as it was for my family.

We like the products made by many companies, but how many do we really have *goodwill* towards? Receiving a share of the rewards (dividends and share value) in companies you buy from and help to build has the potential to create goodwill, just as Bradford & Bingley did for me and my family. Goodwill naturally creates loyalty and increases engagement, something companies spend enormous amounts of money to engender in customers.

University with the middle classes (1998–2001)

I managed to get good GCSE and A-level grades and went on to attend a good university. I wasn't a natural exam passer but getting good grades was non-negotiable for my parents, so I put in a lot of study. My 'hours of work to grade achieved' ratio wasn't great but good grades, ultimately, are what counted.

My brother Bidesh has always been a role model for me. He successfully graduated and then became a chartered accountant at one of the major London firms. When I was at school, I remember him saying to my mum that, instead of being a chartered accountant, he would have preferred to have been a management consultant. There were no professional qualifications with associated exams to take, there was more interesting work, and there was more pay. That sounded good to me, and so from a young age, when most kids wanted to be something fun like a firefighter, I became fixated on becoming a management consultant.

Following my A-levels, I undertook a BSc in Computing and Business Studies at Warwick, a well-regarded university and course, especially for getting into one of the top management consulting firms, which was my dream at the time. Warwick University was a shock to my system in many ways, albeit a positive one. During my childhood in inner-city Leicester, I was mainly surrounded by other first-generation Indian families. Warwick was the opposite as, at the time, students were largely white and middle class. I enjoyed broadening my horizons and meeting new types of people. Socially, I had a great time, especially in my first two years, where, with my new-found freedom, I didn't put in the hours of study needed and unsurprisingly didn't score very high grades. But I rectified that in the third year and managed to graduate with a good grade overall.

Linking this to co-owned. My big takeaway from university was the huge potential of technology to transform business and society. Computing and Business Studies provided a helpful combination of skills and I left excited about applying them to the real world of business. To achieve any change, technology is typically a key enabler and that's certainly the case with co-owned. Economic models are great but technology is often the difference between a good concept and a huge impact.

I wasn't polished enough to get into one of the major consulting firms straight from university but was fortunate enough to get into a smaller, more specialist firm, called Detica (now part of BAE) in a newly formed and rapidly growing financial services consulting practice.

My first professional act (2001–2015)

After graduating from university in 2001, I was a management consultant for around 14 years. I excelled from day one. While academia didn't come naturally to me, business and management consulting did. At Detica, I was fortunate to start my career with Tim Delahunty, a senior manager in the firm and my line manager, and with the late Tim Burfoot, who was the head of the financial services practice. Their early support, guidance and belief in me were invaluable. I remain grateful to this day.

After a couple of years at Detica, I applied and was accepted into one of the major consulting firms and joined PA Consulting, again in its financial services practice, a company that I couldn't get into straight from university.

The aim of consulting is to become a partner in the firm.

Partners are typically extroverted and well networked, as a key part of the role is being able to sell millions of pounds' worth of consulting work each year to banks and financial institutions. I was neither extrovert nor well connected but I had other useful strengths. I realised I was an original thinker and able to gain buy-in for my ideas. Even better, most of the time those ideas turned out to be good ones, benefiting my clients, which led to a virtuous cycle of winning more and more work. In my early thirties, I became the youngest partner globally in the firm, having sold tens of millions of pounds' worth of consulting assignments.

Linking this to co-owned. I worked with around 20 financial institutions during my time in consulting, typically with the executive team, and every project was about one thing: increasing or protecting shareholder value in some form. Almost everyone I worked with, both in consulting and the financial institutions, was obsessed with increasing shareholder value. While delivering for shareholders (ie owners) makes sense, I was always surprised that most people didn't really know, or care, who these mythical shareholders were. I don't mean the names of the institutions but the ultimate beneficial owners (the people who ultimately own or control an asset) behind them. The vast majority of shareholder value goes to people who are already wealthy. Now, I have nothing against wealthy people – in fact I admire a great many – but I struggled with the idea of devoting my life to them without my work delivering a wider, positive social impact.

My second professional act (2015–2023)

In 2015, when I was in my mid-thirties and after becoming a partner at PA Consulting, I had an important decision to make: should I stay in management consulting? I'd put in 14 years of work making it to the top, so shouldn't I stay and reap the rewards? On the other hand, a nagging sense that I could achieve some wider social purpose was pulling me away from my current role. Should I take a leap into the unknown, follow my growing passion and become a social entrepreneur? As I define it, a social entrepreneur is one who focuses as much on delivering a return for society as they do for themselves and their shareholders. They focus their business on solving one of the many big problems in society. It's 'business with social purpose'.

So, I decided that I *would* follow my passion and become a social entrepreneur. However, there were so many pressing issues to solve, I didn't know what type of business I should start. What big problem in society should I pour my efforts into?

Around the same time, I met and married my wife Somita, a surgeon in the NHS. We had our first child, Ayush, and our second, Aarav, was on the way. With me a partner at a consulting firm and Somita a surgeon, our working hours were long and unpredictable. We employed a nanny – let's call her Zara here – to support Ayush and Aarav, and us as a family. As it happens, Zara had some money challenges. These inspired the first business with a social purpose that I went on to set up, called Salary Finance.

After she had been working for a year as our children's nanny, I could see Zara getting more stressed and distracted at work by the day. This wasn't great for anyone. We wanted a happy and engaged nanny looking after our children. Besides that, whatever the issues were, they were obviously stressful and upsetting for her, too. So, one day, I asked her what the issue was and whether we could help. Zara set out her issue clearly: money. I was surprised to hear this, as she was paid well and Somita and I worked hard to afford to pay her well. She went on to explain that the issue wasn't how much she was paid; it was her spiralling debts. We would pay her but much of her money would go towards paying off high interest on her debts such as credit cards and high-interest loans, so she was left with very little to live on. I also had some debt in the form of a low-interest bank loan and asked if I could help her obtain one, to save on the high interest costs. Zara explained that she had a poor credit score so she couldn't get a bank loan and could only borrow money from places offering high interest, causing an endless cycle of debt and stress.

To solve this issue, Somita and I decided to offer Zara a simple solution: an employee loan. We offered her a £2,500 loan at nominal interest so there were no tax implications and we could collect the repayments from her payroll so that the loan would automatically be paid off. She agreed. We gave her the loan on a Friday. By the following Wednesday, Zara was a different person. Her high-interest debts had been paid off. There was no further stress from juggling multiple repayments from multiple debtors and she had more of her own money in her back pocket instead of it immediately going out to pay off high interest. Our loan was quickly repaid, with more income going towards paying off the debt rather than just the interest. Once the loan was repaid, Zara focused on saving, never wanting to get into the same position again.

It was a win for all of us. Zara was less stressed and she kept more of her hard-earned money. Consequently, she did a better job of looking after Ayush and Aarav and was grateful to us as her employer, and therefore more loyal. Besides that, Somita and I felt great about being able to help someone.

One evening, while doing bedtime with Ayush, I had a brainwave. From my experience as a management consultant, I knew Zara's situation was not unique – it was one of those big problems in society that I was hoping to solve. Generally, the more someone earns, the better their credit score and the less interest they'll pay if they need to borrow money. Somita and I were in this category. Conversely, the lower someone's income, typically the lower their credit score. They then pay a higher interest rate and therefore it costs them more to borrow money. Zara fell into this category. The same was true for my family growing up.

This is obviously very regressive: an interest premium for those who earn less creates an endless debt cycle for millions. But, from the banks' and financial institutions' perspective, it's rational: lower-income people with lower credit scores have a higher risk of not making repayments, a cost that's factored in with higher interest rates. I was aware from my work as a management consultant to banks that this was a big issue in society. Banks typically decline two out of three applications for loans, only accepting higher income, higher credit score individuals. High-cost lenders and even illegal lending products fill the gap.

There are millions of working people in Zara's situation: a never-ending debt cycle eats away their income, making it hard to progress in life and impacting them at home and work. The magic of what we'd done for Zara was that we'd made her loan low risk. So, in our model, despite her lower income and lower credit score, we could lend to her at a lower rate of interest in a manner that was still rational.

While Somita and I had solved this problem for our one employee and made a transformational difference to her life, I couldn't help thinking, what if large employers across the country, or even the world, did the same for their employees? Simple employee loans, repaid directly from payroll to reduce the risk, allow a low interest rate and the debt to be paid off sooner, improving employees' home lives and consequently engagement and performance at work. Instead of just a happy Zara, there would be happy millions of working people who find themselves in the same situation – a simple solution to a complex, multi-dimensional societal problem. And so, the idea for my first business with a social purpose was seeded: Salary Finance.

In 2015, I left PA Consulting and joined forces with two co-founders, Daniel Shakhani (a former Goldman Sachs banker) and Dan Cobley (a former Google UK MD) and we raised seed funding for the Salary Finance idea. To launch, we raised seed funding from Blenheim Chalcot, a leading venture builder founded by Manoj Badale and Charles Mindenhall. They have successfully built many ventures over the past 20-plus years, providing their ventures with both capital and strategic and operational support.

Our pitch to employers to join Salary Finance was simple and compelling. We would typically go to the CEOs of the largest employers in the country and set out the problem statement. As an example, I met with Gavin Patterson, the former BT CEO, and explained that if he, or a member of his executive team, needed a loan, they would simply go to a high street bank and would likely be offered a low-interest loan. However, if the same happened to one of his front-line workers (say a call centre employee), they would likely be declined by the high street banks and only have high-interest options available to them, such as credit cards and high-interest lenders. Those high-interest options eat into their already lower income, creating endless cycles of debt and ultimately this impacts their engagement and productivity at work (just as it did for Zara). If we could address this and reduce the interest rate differential between higher- and lower-income employees, it would be the equivalent of a 5 per cent pay rise for much of the workforce. Gavin got it immediately and BT, as many large employers did, rapidly signed up and started seeing huge benefits. Suddenly, the simple employee loan I offered Zara was being offered by large employers across the country through my rapidly growing company Salary Finance.

Another early client, Dunelm, based in my birth city of Leicester, where we knew the chairman, was our first retail client. Immediately after the launch at Dunelm, we saw high take-up of employees taking a Salary Finance loan, typically about £3,000 each, saving them £600 in interest relative to what they were previously paying, becoming debt free six to twelve months sooner and increasing their credit score by 5 per cent on average – Salary Finance reports loan payments to the credit bureaus automatically as part of the payroll process, which means the employee gets an improved score for being reliable. Dunelm's HR team were delighted with the impact on employees and hearing the many employee stories, just like Zara's, of the difference we collectively made to their lives.

The model worked economically, too. We made the same return per loan as a bank would but we could lend to lower-income employees with lower credit scores. As well as helping their employees, companies joining Salary Finance were seeing improvements across other people metrics, such as a 27 per cent reduction in employee turnover among Salary Finance users, as we reduced money worries and created goodwill with employees. It's a win–win model that achieved explosive growth and impact and has become the poster child among fintech (financial technology) businesses with social purpose, a movement we have been at the forefront of.

Nine years on, in an industry that didn't previously

exist, Salary Finance now serves a community of more than five million employees in the UK and more than ten million employees in the US. In the UK, we partner with 20 per cent of the FTSE 100, eight of the ten largest supermarkets and retailers (including Tesco, the largest employer in the country), two in three hospital trusts, and employers covering almost every sector. Ironically, we also work with many banks, whose own front-line employees (eg in the branch or call centre) are declined for a loan by their own bank employer due to low credit scores. In the US, we work with more than 500,000 companies, from four employees in size to 400,000, including household name companies such as Tesla, Comcast and Samsung. From my one loan to Zara, we have now funded billions of pounds/dollars in employee loans and expanded what we do to include a broader set of financial employee benefits offered exclusively through the workplace, such as payroll-deducted savings and financial education.

To achieve this, we have raised more than £100 million in equity from investors, including Legal and General, Blenheim Chalcot, Goldman Sachs, Experian and Royal London. We've also raised hundreds of millions in debt to fund loans from financial institutions, including JP Morgan and Virgin Money. To build the company, we've also hired more than 500 people in the Salary Finance team across the UK, US and India since we launched in 2015.

Salary Finance has won more than 70 awards for its work, including from Business in the Community (BITC), one of The Prince's Charities supported by King Charles, which awarded us the highly regarded Socially Responsible Business of the Year. We were also recognised by Deloitte as the 19th-fastest-growing tech company in the UK and by the *Financial Times* as the 44th-fastest-growing tech company in Europe, based on three years of audited accounts.

Salary Finance is also a case study at Harvard Business School on how a big problem in society can be solved through an economic model that serves both shareholders and society. This is a source of particular pride for me (and my mum), as I always wanted to study at Harvard but didn't have the funds to do so, so it's a privilege to now attend as a guest speaker discussing a case study on a business I founded. Salary Finance is now a big, established business, valued at hundreds of millions of pounds. It's set up to do even more great things, giving me the opportunity to start my third act.

Linking this to co-owned. Salary Finance spearheaded a movement in companies who realised that if they could help their employees to improve their financial health, it's good for both the business and its employees. Similarly, for co-owned, the intention is to spearhead a movement in companies who realise that if they can help their customers improve their financial health, it's good for both the business and its customers. Naturally, I learned a lot while building Salary Finance, which I'm excited to take forward to Co-owned (see below).

The observant among you will note that I describe myself as a 'serial' social entrepreneur, meaning I've done it more than once. While at Salary Finance, I also founded another tech business in the UK called Work Report. This leveraged the relationships we'd built with payroll providers through Salary Finance to form a consortium with them and build APIs (ie common data bridges) with their data, which enabled consumers to easily get digital access to their own payroll data and share it securely with third parties of their choice. For example, when moving house and needing to verify employment and income, this could be done digitally, securely and instantly through the Work Report API, rather than having to request a letter from an employer. It would also allow, for example, those with no or low credit scores to easily provide supplementary employment and income data to improve their chances of getting access to products that otherwise required a high credit score. Work Report, at the time of writing, has built connectivity to payroll providers that covers 80 per cent of the UK's working population. Employment and income verification is big business in the US, with Equifax, one of the major credit bureaus, earning more than $1 billion revenue annually on it, but no one had gained traction in the UK. Dann Adams, a former executive at Equifax in the US and now a friend, was a big fan of Salary Finance and saw the opportunity to extend what we did to this new area. He introduced the idea to me, so we built the product rapidly and within 18 months it was acquired by Experian, the other major credit bureau.

Alongside Salary Finance and Work Report, I'm also chair of the largest non-profit in the UK (possibly in the world) focused on the financial education of young people, called MyBnk. The organisation has delivered financial education to more than 350,000 young people in partnership with more than 1,000 schools, youth organisations and local authorities and helps young people learn the rules of money management early in life.

An example of one of MyBnk's flagship programmes is The Money House. This helps vulnerable young people – often brought up in social care and about to move into independent housing – manage their money and maintain their first rental property tenancy. Interactive sessions take place over the course of a week, sometimes in a real house, where MyBnk trainers teach real-life skills for the real world. Participants gain practical, financial and digital skills to help them learn about, for example, tenancy agreements (rights and responsibilities and cost of moving in), avoiding eviction (paying household bills and rent on time), banking (accounts, savings, credit cards and how to borrow safely), budgeting and spending habits (including consumer rights), benefits (entitlements and universal credit) and energy efficiency (coping with rising living costs). We explain how they can make informed choices about their future and teach them how to best manage their money, ultimately to prevent homelessness, which is common among care leavers (MyBnk nd).

The impact has been profound. A survey found that 14 per cent of young people leaving social care have, at some point, been homeless following an eviction from their first independent living experience (Gill & Daw 2017). For attendees of MyBnk's Money House, this reduces to less than 2 per cent. We teach them the rules of the game in an engaging way and this creates positive money habits.

Linking this to co-owned. While financial education has a poor reputation in terms of efficacy and impact, if it's delivered in an engaging way that changes behaviours and creates positive habits, it has the potential for enormous social change at scale. This is an area in which MyBnk is leading the charge for young people. It too raises millions from many leading financial institutions as it scales its work and impact. Co-owned has the potential to educate the common person about investments in a safe and engaging way, through receiving shares as they go about their day-to-day spending.

My third professional act (2023 onwards)

Launching this book as well as Co-owned, a research and technology organisation aiming to help companies on their path to becoming co-owned, is my third professional act. It's the most important yet and brings together everything I've experienced and learned so far. I've come from an upbringing in a low-income, first-generation immigrant household, watching my mum managing the tightest of budgets but still finding money to save and invest, to rising through the ranks as a management consultant and learning about how major institutions are run, primarily for the benefit of their shareholders (an important but small proportion of society). From there I went on to launch Salary Finance and prove that business and social impact can go hand in hand, at scale, with the backing of major financial institutions, and to my work with MyBnk and experiencing the transformational impact financial education can have if it's delivered in an engaging way that changes behaviours and habits.

Rather than in the form of a slide presentation, I've decided to start my third professional act with this book. This is because the challenges of capitalism are multifaceted and complex and a book provides the opportunity to explain my thinking in detail. Besides that, transformational change requires a collective movement. This book is designed to inspire others to join me on this journey. I hope that, by the time you've finished reading it, you'll feel inspired to become a part of it.

3

The fundamental issue with capitalism today

*Capitalism made it possible to become
wealthy by serving your fellow man.*
– Walter Williams, American economist

C o-owned is a logical growth idea for big business. As set out in Chapter 1, an almost universal truth in business is that long-term success is typically linked to the loyalty and engagement of customers. Making customers co-owners, if implemented in a practical and effective way, has the potential to improve loyalty and engagement, leading to higher returns for all (shareholders and customer co-owners).

The thinking underpinning co-owned is, however, much deeper than a new business growth idea in isolation. Co-owned is intended to course-correct capitalism, enabling economic growth that lifts both the common person as well as shareholders. Without it, I fear we're heading to deeper mass impoverishment and mass social unrest that will impact generations to come.

This chapter looks at the wider economic context and why I believe capitalism in its current form is no longer working for society. It's quite data and chart heavy because I believe it's important for business leaders to engage with this wider economic context, not just the realities of their business in isolation. No business is immune to macro-economic trends and those that perform the best in the long term are typically those that can respond to these trends ahead of time. This chapter is intended to help leaders reflect on their businesses in terms of that wider economic context, how capitalism is playing out today, why it's not sustainable and what it could mean for their business longer term.

The benefits of capitalism

Capitalism faces unprecedented challenges and criticisms. But as an economic system, it has many benefits. I am, personally, a fan. I prefer it to high levels of state intervention, regulation and high taxation and spending. Of course, in most capitalist economies, there's some necessary government intervention but the overarching economic system is still one of capitalism. Still, while I'm a fan of capitalism, I don't think it's working for the common person today. In developing the concept of co-owned, my aim is to help big business make the benefits of capitalism more inclusive and, as a result, make the wider economic system more sustainable.

Before deep-diving into where capitalism is failing and where I think big business must act, I've set out some of the benefits at the core of capitalism because, in trying to steer capitalism in a new direction, we shouldn't throw the baby out with the bathwater.

Capitalism's core principles include private ownership, free markets and competition. This has served as a catalyst for economic growth around the world. Entrepreneurship and the pursuit of profit have fuelled innovation and investment, leading to the creation of new industries and the growth of existing ones. Capitalism incentivises risk-taking and rewards those who succeed, providing individuals and businesses with the motivation to constantly improve and meet the evolving demands of consumers.

Capitalism also creates an environment conducive to research, development and the commercialisation of new ideas. The profit-driven nature of capitalism stimulates companies to invest in research and development, resulting in breakthroughs across diverse fields such as computing, telecommunications, biotechnology and many others. These advancements have revolutionised industries, increased productivity and enhanced quality of life for people across the globe. This doesn't take away the role, or the benefits, of government investment in research and development, as in the way that the US government underwrote Silicon Valley. But the point remains that capitalism plays a key role in the ecosystem.

Capitalism has also facilitated the growth of global trade, creating interconnected economies and enabling countries to specialise in areas where they have a comparative advantage. Free trade agreements have facilitated the exchange of goods and services, empowering nations to tap into global markets and reap the rewards of international commerce.

Where capitalism is failing

So, I believe there's a lot to like about capitalism. But despite this, I fear that it's essentially broken as an economic system that lifts society as a whole. It's analogous to a bank. A bank can operate for many years even when there are fundamental issues that are negatively affecting it. Then suddenly, when things unravel, it can fail in a matter of days, if not hours – Hemingway's 'gradually, then suddenly'. After decades of gradual decline in the benefits of capitalism, we're now in the 'sudden' downfall phase. Why?

Over the past three decades, since the 1980s, we've seen various trends. Note that I use the term *trends*, as there are, of course, many factors that impact numbers year to year and quarter to quarter, but the following trends are clear to see in the data.

Here are five things that have been *rising* over the past three decades:

→ **Employment:** a higher percentage of the population is working.

→ **Economic growth:** GDP is growing with increased consumption of goods and services.

→ **Stock prices:** public companies are rising in value through growing sales and profit margins.

→ **Investor-funded (eg private equity-owned) companies:** more companies are owned by financial investors, which are becoming more valuable.

→ **Corporate profits:** big companies make higher profits, driven by a growing economy (more consumption of goods and services) and higher profit margins.

Despite all the above, there's one thing that hasn't been rising: real wages – and consequently standards of living and wealth, unless you are in the top 1 per cent of earners, where compensation is typically linked to profits or share price (both of which have been rising). This begs an important question: if the rewards of economic growth are not seen in increasing workers' real wages, where is it going? It's going to shareholders, who represent a small proportion of society and are now the ultimate beneficiaries of economic growth, which manifests itself through increased corporate profits and share value.

Has it always been like this? No. It started to diverge in the 1980s. In the decades after the Second World War, there was income and wealth inequality, a necessary by-product of capitalism, but all parts of society grew somewhat proportionally, with growth in real wages and consequently standards of living as well as growth in shareholder returns. However, this stopped in the 1980s. Real wages stopped growing but economic growth, corporate profits and share price growth continued (look back to Figure 1).

There has also been another, linked consumer trend. The common person's savings and investments rates have been declining, creating significant financial fragility. The common person typically no longer partakes in the wealth creation of the economy, which is primarily realised through investment (shareholder) gains. The common person lives off wages, which on average see no growth in real terms, while their continued spending and consumption fuels a growing economy, corporate profits and share prices, which continue to drive more and more wealth for shareholders.

Wealth inequality grows at a higher rate than income inequality. This is partly because there are lower taxes on capital (investment gains) vs income and, as the saying goes, it's easier to make money from money. For example, at the time of writing, high interest rates are creating pressure on the finances of the common person through mortgages and indirectly on rents but creating a healthy return for those with savings. Increasing wages alone won't solve mass impoverishment; there's a need to increase the wealth of the common person too. The current situation is creating an economic system in freefall, one that works for shareholders but not the common person. The rest of this chapter provides the data and charts informing this viewpoint before we go on to how to course-correct in a manner that preserves the benefits of capitalism.

The data and trends

Rising employment

Since the 1980s, the number of people employed in the US has been steadily increasing (also supported by population growth) from 99 million working people in 1980 to 158 million working people in 2022 (Figure 2). The unemployment rate has fluctuated based on recessions but with a downward trend, from 7.18 per cent in 1980 to 3.64 per cent in 2022.

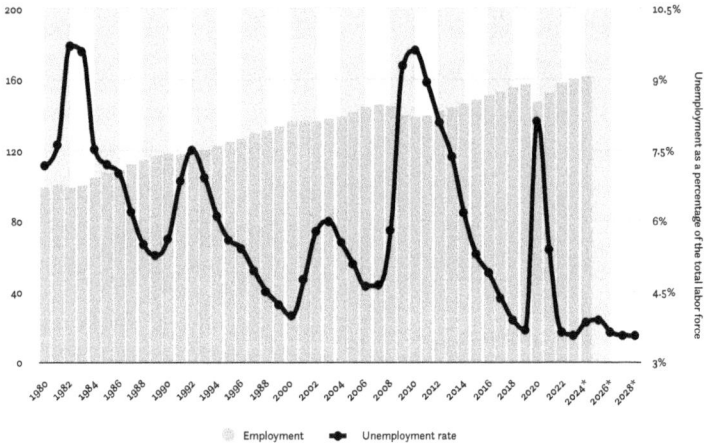

Figure 2: Total employment and unemployment rate in the United States from 1980 to 2022, with projections until 2028

This trend is also consistent in the UK (Figure 3), with the employment rate increasing from 71.7 per cent in 1980 to 75.9 per cent in 2022.

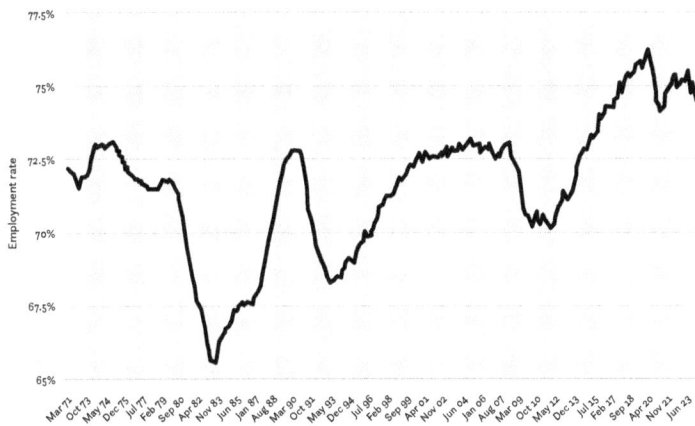

Figure 3: Employment rate in the United Kingdom from March 1971 to June 2023

Rising economic growth

Gross domestic product has increased steadily in the US since the 1980s, as more workers consume more goods and services, growing from $4.8 trillion in 1987 to $23 trillion in 2021 (Figure 4).

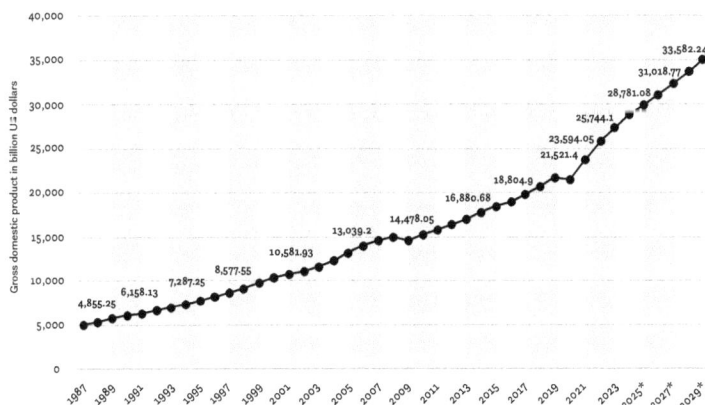

Figure 4: Gross domestic product (GDP) of the United States at current prices from 1987 to 2029 (projected) in billion US dollars

The same trend is again true in the UK (Figure 5), but with periods of declining growth in recessions, with overall GDP growing from $0.8 trillion in 1988 to $3.1 trillion in 2022. The shape of the US and UK chart trends are almost identical on a per capita basis.

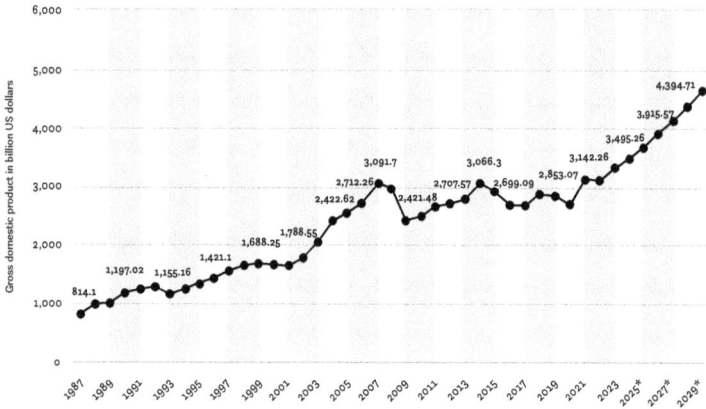

Figure 5: Gross domestic product (GDP) in current prices of the United Kingdom (UK) from 1987 to 2029 (in billion US dollars)

Rising stock prices

The S&P (Standard and Poor's) 500 is a stock market index tracking the stock performance of 500 of the largest companies listed on stock exchanges in the United States. Its trend has also been upwards, excluding periods of recession, growing from 164 in 1983 to 4,200 in 2021 (Figure 6).

Similarly in the UK, the FTSE 100, the index composed of the 100 largest (by market capitalisation) companies listed on the London Stock Exchange (LSE), grew from 1,096 in 1984 to 7,022 in 2022 (Figure 7).

Figure 6: S&P 500 index by year. Source: Refinitiv by the New York Times

Figure 7: FTSE 100 index by year

Rising investor-funded (eg private equity-owned) companies

Outside of public companies listed on stock exchanges, private companies owned by private equity (financial investors) have also grown rapidly in the US, from assets of less than $1 trillion in 2000 to more than $7 trillion in 2020 (Figure 8).

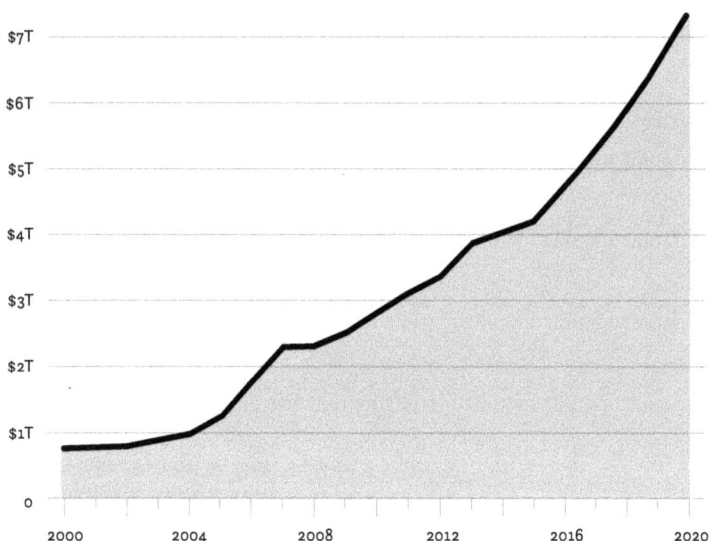

Figure 8: Assets managed by private equity. Source: Mother Jones

Similarly in the UK, the market size of companies owned by private equity has grown steadily, from £1.8 trillion in 2012 to £3.1 trillion in 2022 (Figure 9).

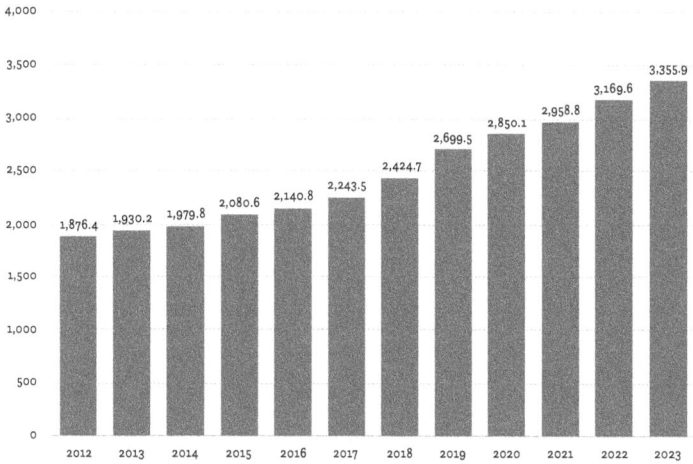

Figure 9: Market size of the private equity (PE) industry in the United Kingdom (UK) from 2012 to 2022 with a forecast for 2023 (in million GBP)

Rising corporate profits

In 2021, corporations in the US made profits of around $2.77 trillion. This represents significant growth since 2000, when corporate profits totalled $786 billion (Figure 10). The corporate profits are defined as the net income of corporations in the national income and product accounts (NIPA).

The same trend applies in the UK (Figure 11). Gross profit by UK private non-financial companies was £2.9 trillion in 2016, up from circa £1.5 trillion in 1997.

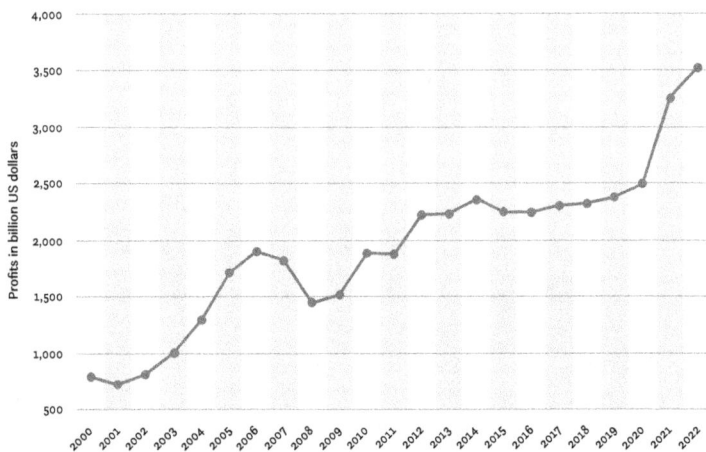

Figure 10: *Corporate profits in the United States from 2000 to 2022 (in billion US dollars)*

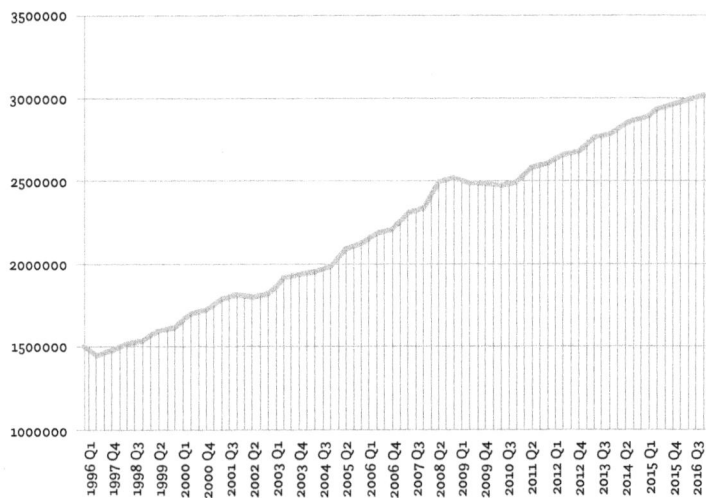

Figure 11: *Gross profit by UK non-financial companies*

Stagnant real wages

Despite the rises in company valuations and profits, average real wages (offsetting for inflation) have been broadly flat in the US, at circa $23 per hour (Figure 12).

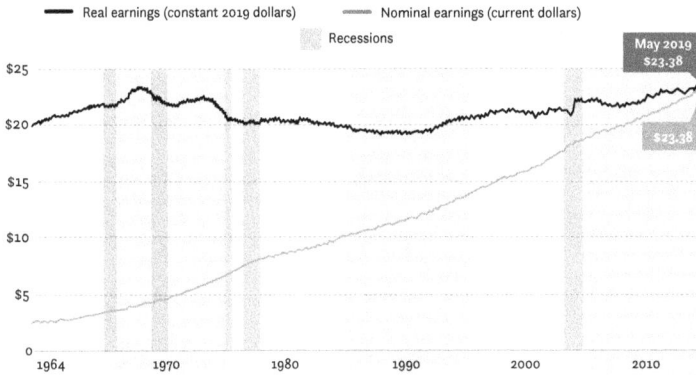

Figure 12: Average hourly US earnings

This excludes the top 1 per cent, where real wage growth is typically linked to share value or profits, which have been growing (Figure 13, showing UK figures).

Similarly in the UK, while there was growth in real wages between 2000 and 2008, the past 14 years have netted out to broadly flat real wages in the period (Figure 14).

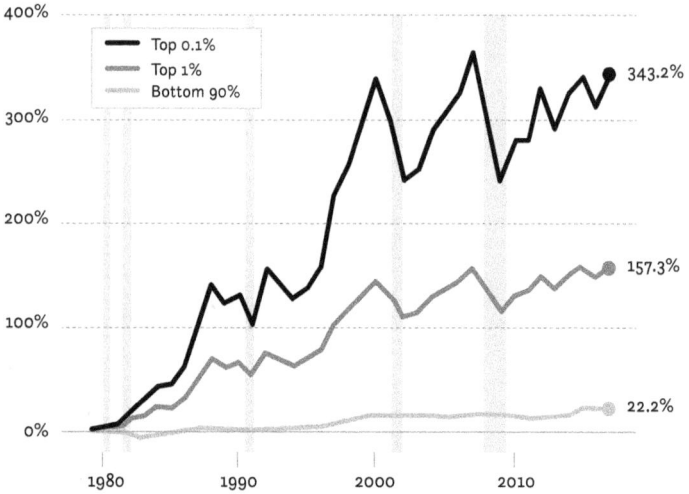

Figure 13: Cumulative per cent change in real earnings by earnings group, 1979–2017

Figure 14: UK real consumer pay

Economic gains

With economic gains going to shareholders (company owners) in the form of corporate profits and share prices and not to workers, who are the shareholders? In 1989, the wealthiest 1 per cent of Americans owned 39 per cent of the stock market. By 2016, this had grown to 50 per cent. The wealthiest 10 per cent of Americans now own 92 per cent of the stock market, compared to the least wealthy 50 per cent, who only own 0.25 per cent of the stock market (Figure 15).

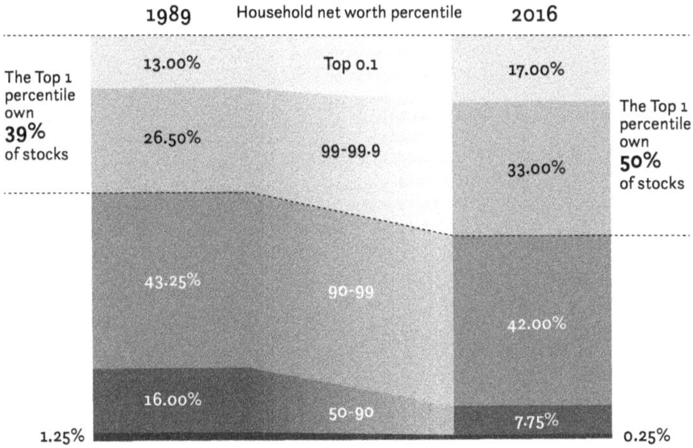

Figure 15: US stock market ownership by wealth category

Figure 16 (from the *New York Times*, based on Federal Reserve Board survey data) paints a similar picture.

Families grouped by percentiles of net worth:

	Share of Families	Overall Equities	Directly Held Stock
Bottom 50	50%	1%	0%
50 to 80	30%	6%	3%
80 to 90	10%	9%	4%
90 to 95	5%	13%	7%
95 to 99	4%	33%	34%
99 to 100	1%	38%	51%

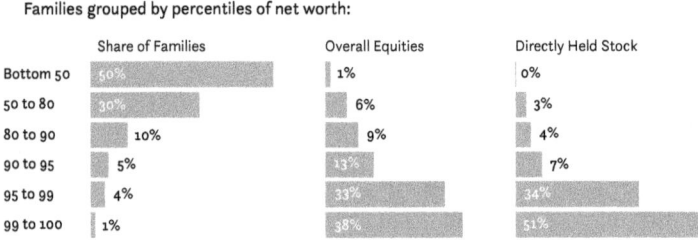

Figure 16: When the stock market rises, so does inequality

While the same chart is not available in the UK, the trend is materially the same as in the US. In the UK, there has been a declining ownership of company shareholdings from resident individuals from 54 per cent in 1963 to just over 10 per cent in 2019 (Figure 17).

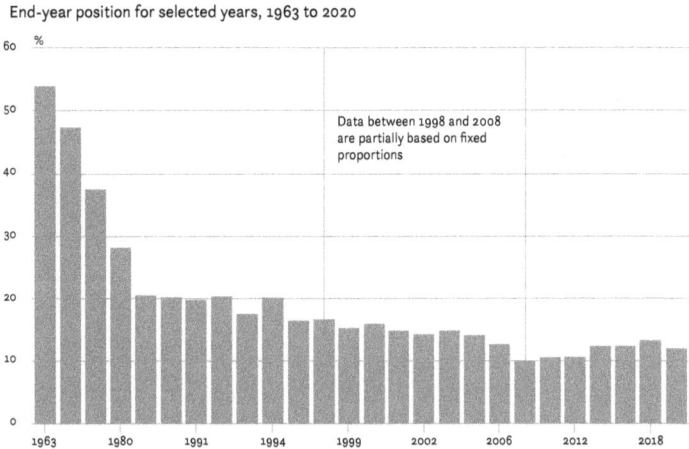

End-year position for selected years, 1963 to 2020

Data between 1998 and 2008 are partially based on fixed proportions

Figure 17: UK-resident individuals' shareholdings

Furthermore, in the UK, beneficial owners of UK listed companies are now dominated by non-UK residents (ie not workers) and financial institutions (Figure 18).

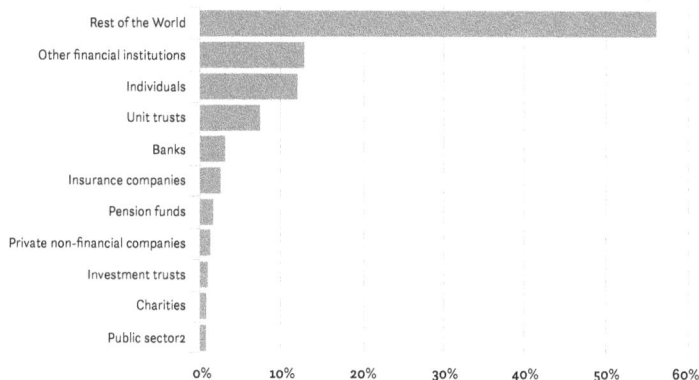

Figure 18: Beneficial owners of UK quoted shares

The divergence of economic growth and real wages

I've already shared Figure 1 – see page 4 – which shows that, after World War Two, economic growth and wages grew in parallel. Then, in the 1980s, they started to diverge, as the incremental economic growth was no longer being realised through increased wages but through increased profits and shareholder gains.

Furthermore, Figure 19 shows that after WW2 and up to 1980, while there was income inequality, economic growth lifted all income categories reasonably proportionally.

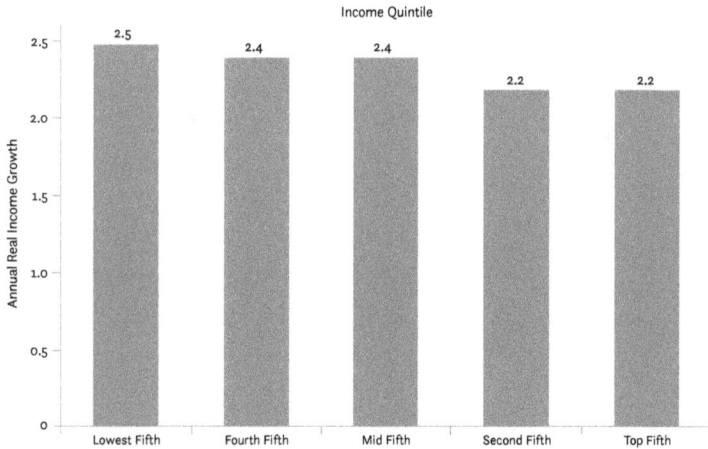

Figure 19: Real US family income growth 1947–1979

This fell apart from the 1980s, as income growth rapidly increased for the top fifth, while reducing for the bottom fifth, as can be seen in Figure 20.

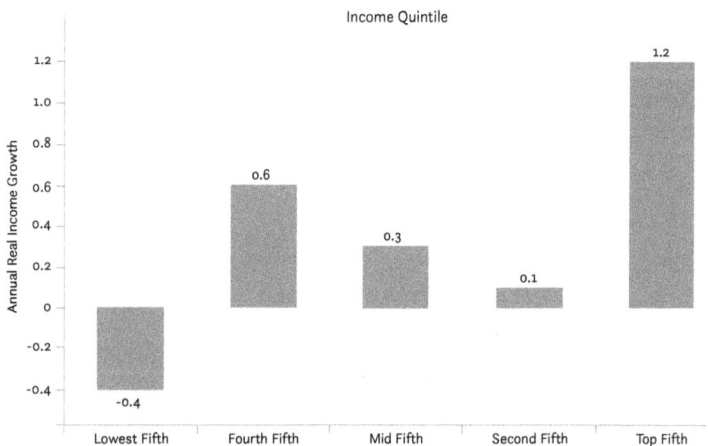

Figure 20: Real US family income growth 1979–2010

The same can be seen in the UK, with the gap of wealth distribution between the bottom 50 per cent and top 10 per cent closing until the mid-1980s, after which it starts to widen (Figure 21).

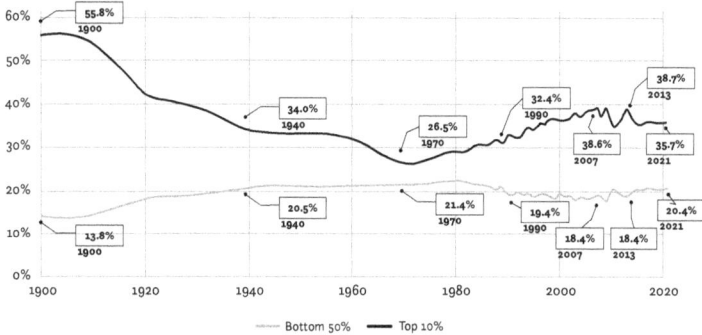

Figure 21: Wealth distribution in the UK

Savings and investment rates of the general population

Another issue is the level of savings (and financial health) of the general population in the UK and US. We saw in Chapter 2 how many people have no savings at all – or only a very small amount. This is a good representation of what mass impoverishment looks like today – almost half of the population of the United States can't afford to replace their boiler should it break.

Wealth inequality grows at a higher rate than income inequality

While the lack of growth in real wages has been an issue, the bigger consequential issue is the impact on wealth. On a global basis, Figure 22 shows that, from an income perspective, the least wealthy 50 per cent account for 8.5

per cent of the world's income, with the most wealthy 10 per cent accounting for 52 per cent of the world's income. However, from a wealth perspective, the situation is even more polarised. The least wealthy 50 per cent in the world hold only 2 per cent of global wealth, compared to the most wealthy 10 per cent, who account for 76 per cent of global wealth.

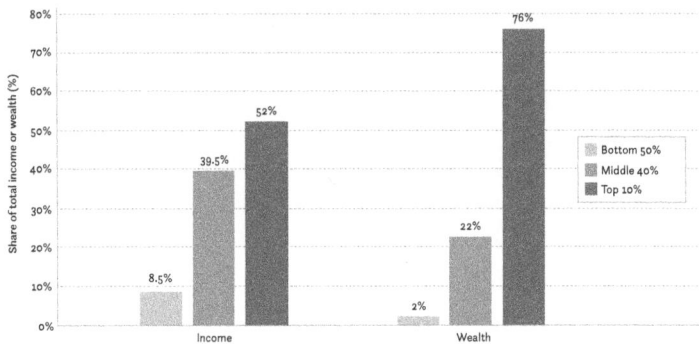

Figure 22: Global income and wealth inequality, 2021

The greater concentration of wealth, relative to income, is caused by investment returns from wealth having a lower tax burden (capital gains tax is lower than income tax) and also wealth accruing from compound returns, for example returns by investing in the stock market and reinvesting gains. In the UK, as set out in Figure 23, there's now a x875 difference in the wealth between the most and least wealthy 10 per cent.

The top 10% of households are 875 times wealthier than those at the bottom

Top 10% of households

Bottom 10% of households

Figure 23: Wealth inequality in the UK

Conclusion

Capitalism works for shareholders, the primary beneficiaries of economic growth – but it no longer works for the common person, who has seen no growth in real wages or living standards in several decades. They don't benefit from economic growth despite their hand in creating it through their labour and consumption of goods and services, both of which drive shareholder profits and returns. No real wage growth, coupled with a culture of consumption (instead of saving and investing) and the rising cost of living (food, energy, housing), means that we're in freefall when it comes to inequality. While inequality itself isn't the issue, as some degree of inequality has always been a necessary by-product of capitalism, the continual and growing mass impoverishment of the common person is. To create a harmonious society that every human values (shareholder or common person), we must find a way of lifting the common person off the current negative flywheel – a flywheel that leads not to small, incremental wins but to deeper and deeper impoverishment.

4

Introducing co-owned and its aims

Innovation and commerce are as powerful tools for creating social progress as they are for driving technological advancement.
– Kiran Mazumdar-Shaw, Indian entrepreneur

The aim of co-owned is to realign capitalism, not reinvent it. Capitalism, as set out in the last chapter, has many benefits and has enabled much progress in the world. However, as with all systems, to stand the test of time and to remain relevant and valid, there's a need for innovation. Co-owned represents a much-needed innovation for capitalism. This chapter homes in on the problem co-owned is solving and why it is the answer.

What's the problem we're solving?

In summary, capitalism in today's world, particularly in the US and UK, is characterised by the following:

- More and more workers work and get paid.
- Worker wages remain largely stagnant year after year in average real terms.
- Workers spend their stagnant real wages on goods and services with a culture of consumption that's prioritised above saving, investing and wealth creation.
- This spending drives company profits, the ultimate beneficial owners of which are share-holders, a relatively small group in society.
- This repeats every pay cycle, with workers in a growing state of mass impoverishment and shareholders growing in wealth.

While not all workers are equal – there are of course higher-paid workers and those who are able to save, invest and build wealth, but they're in the minority. For the common person, social mobility is at best stagnant, personal debt is at record levels and growing, and access to the basics of life such as affordable housing is increasingly out of reach.

The following data point, I believe, tells us that capitalism is now reaching breaking point. In 2020, CNN ran a news story headlined 'Millennials are worse off than their parents – a first in American history' (Luhby 2020). This is a huge red flag. Generations going backwards in wealth must be addressed with seriousness and urgency.

There are now numerous studies and research papers that have examined the financial situation of Millennials compared to their parents' generation, consistently highlighting the growing wealth disparity. Some of the studies and their findings are summarised below. While the conclusions are the same, the breadth of the studies signifies the importance of the results and why I believe we've reached breaking point.

US Federal Reserve data: A study of the Federal Reserve's Survey of Consumer Finances in 2019 found that Millennials have lower levels of wealth compared to previous generations at the same age. Adjusted for inflation, the median net worth of Millennials aged 35–44 was 20 per cent lower than that of both Baby Boomers and Generation X at the same age (Colley 2023).

Deloitte's Millennial survey: Deloitte's global survey in 2018 revealed that only 43 per cent of Millennials expected to be better off financially than their parents. This marked a significant decline from previous surveys, indicating a growing pessimism about their future financial prospects.

Pew Research Center analysis: Pew Research Center conducted an analysis (Bialik & Fry 2019) which showed that the median net worth of Millennials in the US was approximately 20 per cent less than that of Generation X at the same age, and around 40 per cent less than that of Baby Boomers. The research highlighted the impact of economic factors such as income inequality, the Great Recession and the burden of student loan debt on Millennials' wealth accumulation.

Young Invincibles report: A report by Young Invincibles, a non-profit organisation, also corroborated that millennial households have significantly lower net worth than previous generations at similar life stages (Allison 2018). In 2018 it found that the net wealth of Millennials was half that of Baby Boomers at the same age.

Institute for Fiscal Studies (IFS) study: In the UK, the IFS conducted research that again showed Millennials had accumulated significantly less wealth than previous generations (Sturrock 2023).

Common themes in these studies are the impact of rising house prices, increasing student debt and lower home-ownership rates on Millennials' wealth.

These studies, among others, support the growing reality that Millennials are the first generation in recent history to be less wealthy than their parents at the same age. And given the negative flywheel set out at the end of the previous chapter, this trend is getting worse every day, as the common person becomes more and more impoverished.

I've used the term 'mass impoverishment' a number of times. This refers to a condition where a significant portion of the population experiences a significant decline in their overall economic wellbeing, leading to a state of widespread poverty and diminished living standards. It suggests a situation where a large number of individuals or households face increasing financial hardship, often characterised by reduced income, limited access to basic necessities, decreased social mobility and a lack of economic opportunities. Mass impoverishment reflects a systemic failure in addressing socioeconomic inequalities and can have far-reaching consequences for individuals, communities and society as a whole. Mark E. Thomas describes mass impoverishment as 'a process of levelling-down amongst all but the wealthy' (Thomas 2021).

You could argue that we're not technically at this stage in the UK or US. However, if current trends continue it's likely only a matter of time. What's especially concerning about this situation is that mass impoverishment typically takes place in a recession or other economic hardship, such as a war. As we saw in the previous chapter, the past three decades have delivered high economic growth and corporate profits. As a result, it is even more worrying that, in these times of economic growth, we have the first generation in recent history becoming less, not more, affluent. This is a flashing red light.

I struggle to envision a future where the common person vs shareholder dynamic continues to play out and we all live together as a society in harmony. As much as any other humans, shareholders value living in a world where there is social harmony. Unless we solve the mass impoverishment of the common person, the future won't be bright or harmonious for anyone.

What caused the problem?

Despite popular opinion, my experiences lead me to conclude that the problems with capitalism today aren't due to 'greedy shareholders'. Instead, we have shareholders who are acting rationally and broadly within the rules of the system, on a decision-by-decision basis. The collective impact of all these individually rational decisions on the wider macroeconomic and social system has got us to where we are today.

Academically, there are two schools of thought about the purpose of a large corporation and how its key decisions should be governed. There is stakeholder capitalism, where the corporation has a duty to all stakeholders, including workers, consumers, government, environment and shareholders; and there is shareholder capitalism, where there's one purpose only – to maximise shareholder value.

This is characterised by the following quotes:

[Americans] regard business management as a stewardship, and they expect it to operate the economy as a public trust for the benefit of all the people.
– paper and pulp executive J D Zellerbach, quoted in *Time* magazine in 1956 and representing the predominant thinking in the 1940s to 1970s.

Versus these separate statements by billionaire US investor Carl Icahn, representing the predominant thinking from the 1980s onwards:

- ➡ 'We have bloated bureaucracies in Corporate America'
- ➡ 'I have to look out for the shareholder's interests, and I'm the largest shareholder.'

Practically, Icahn's view prevails today. While there have been considerable gains made in CSR (corporate social responsibility) and ESG (environmental, social and governance) practices, the reality is that maximising profits and share price are the predominant factors in corporate strategy and governance today. The management of a firm is, by law, accountable to shareholders. Shareholders hold management to account based on clear metrics that drive shareholder value, such as next quarter earnings.

I have sat on many boards. While CSR and ESG get more airtime, I've never seen a decision approved that would benefit CSR or ESG objectives over shareholder value. This isn't a criticism. It's not even necessarily a negative. But it is a reality essential to acknowledge if we're to put forward new solutions. Put another way, while there are many CSR and ESG decisions and initiatives that positively influence the world, they only happen if they support (or at least do not detract) shareholder value. One example of this is the increase in share buybacks. This is where a company uses its profits or capital to buy its own shares. US share buybacks hit a global record last year (2022) of $1.3 trillion, triple the level of ten years ago (Chisholm 2023). While US companies remain the biggest buyers, these transactions have also grown rapidly in the UK.

One of the primary reasons for share buybacks is to increase the share price, the beneficiaries of which are the executives – whose pay is typically linked to share price – and shareholders. Alternative uses of the capital include, for example, investing in workers' pay. However, there remains very little economic rationale for shareholders to do so beyond the minimum necessary to maintain target employee retention and productivity metrics. So, collectively, given a choice between increasing pay in real terms for workers (amid a global cost of living crisis) or using

$1.2 trillion to buy shares to drive share price, collectively shareholders and executives chose the latter. Why? Because it benefits them as shareholders and executives. They're the rules of the game and their duty under shareholder capitalism (see Figure 24).

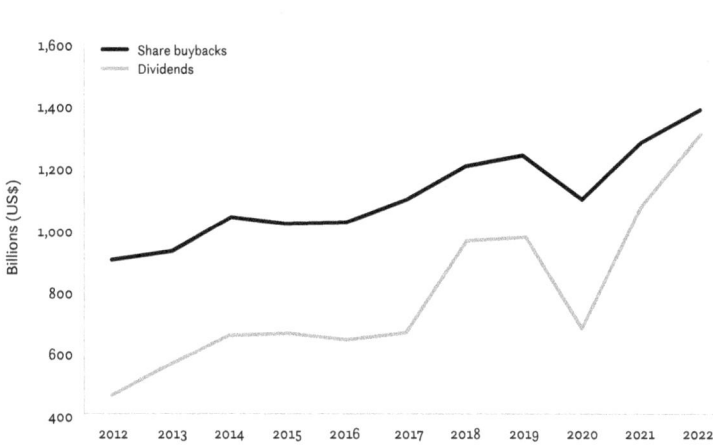

Figure 24: Share buybacks vs dividends

In summary, shareholders act in their own interests. They focus on delivering shareholder value (dividends and share price) to reward their investment and the risks they have taken. There's little rational incentive for them to do otherwise. This drives decisions such as workers' pay, which makes economic sense in isolation but collectively at a systemic economic level has the potential to bring the system down.

Why hasn't the problem been solved?

You might be wondering, if this is such a big issue, why have successive governments in the UK and US failed to address it? Again, it's worth reflecting on this before we set out a solution. I suspect the answer lies somewhere in the following.

Political influence: Shareholders are the wealthiest people in our society. Relatively few people become wealthy from income alone. Naturally, directly or indirectly, these individuals hold political influence – whether that be through, for example, lobbying politicians or making political campaign contributions. This influence can shape policy decisions in their favour.

Neoliberal ideology: Over the past few decades, both the UK and US have embraced neoliberal economic ideologies, emphasising free markets, deregulation and limited government intervention. This ideology prioritises economic growth (which has been happening) and efficiency over addressing discontent among the common people.

Tax policies: The tax system plays an important role and typically favours shareholders. Lower tax rates on capital gains and inheritance and loopholes in the tax codes have allowed shareholders to accumulate and retain more wealth. Reforms to make the tax system more progressive or close loopholes would be considered high risk politically, as they would directly impact the wealthy who, one way or another, fund political parties.

Globalisation and economic forces: The forces of globalisation, including international trade and capital flows, have contributed to wealth concentration. For example, offshoring jobs can reduce the need to increase wages in the UK and US, as the increase is harder to justify to shareholders when the work can be completed at a lower cost in other countries, increasing shareholder returns.

The traditional approach to addressing wealth inequality requires a comprehensive government-led approach that encompasses policy reforms, taxation changes, investment in social programmes and a shift in societal values towards more equitable distribution of wealth, together with international cooperation. Personally, I think this is unlikely and an alternative solution is required: a capitalist solution to a problem within capitalism.

Introducing the customer co-ownership economy (co-owned)

Co-owned is designed to course-correct capitalism by solving the simultaneous challenges of:

- increasing the wealth of the common person, without...
- taking away wealth from the shareholder class and reducing their incentives to invest in economic growth, while...
- helping the common person learn about the benefits of saving, investing, wealth creation and creating positive financial habits; with the added bonus of...
- adding more democracy into how big corporations are governed, given their role and impact in society.

This is a difficult set of challenges to address simultaneously, which is why capitalism is where it is now.

When designing the co-owned model, there are some important principles that I also kept in mind:

- not vilifying any group (shareholders or the common person)
- building on the economic growth success of shareholder capitalism
- finding a solution that both the common person and shareholders want and can see the benefit of.

All of this led me to co-owned. I did start by considering an 'employee co-ownership economy' where more companies offer more shares to their employees but there are some fundamental challenges in evidencing rapid return for shareholders. It's definitely not a zero-sum game, with studies that point to employee co-owned companies being more valuable (Dudley & Rouen 2021b). However, *customers* can drive shareholder value more directly, more quickly and more demonstrably. I'm certainly supportive of employee ownership but here I'm focusing my attention on customer co-ownership, which I think is the bigger and faster way to evidence solutions.

Co-owned is a simple solution to a complex, multi-dimensional set of challenges within capitalism. In the co-owned model, company executives and shareholders proactively:

- issue at least 10 per cent of their shares to their customers (either through issuing new shares or buying existing shares)
- create a broader shareholder base, including retail customer co-shareholders
- drive increased loyalty and engagement from customers
- improve financial metrics (cost of customer

acquisition, lifetime customer value, profitability) and share price, as customers are what ultimately drive value in companies.

Customers can take part as they receive shares (with associated value and dividends) easily and for free in companies they ordinarily buy from and use. They naturally learn about how investing works, with co-owned intended to be the start of their investment habit, which they can then build on in the future. And as an added benefit, customers can vote in key company decisions, with more democracy in corporate decision making through, for example, digital annual general meetings. This represents a rare but resounding win for shareholders, a win for customers and a win for society.

The initial focus for Co-owned is business-to-consumer (B2C) companies, both public and private companies backed by financial investors (private equity and venture capital). There's also a potential application in business-to-business (B2B) companies, which will be developed in a later phase.

Dann Adams on his one share in Disney

In developing the thinking underpinning Co-owned, I spoke to several people whose opinion I really value, from leading professors and personal finance experts to company executives and shareholders. Their input, challenge and support have created a better output and given me a huge amount of confidence in the potential of Co-owned. One of those people is Dann Adams, a former executive at Equifax, one of the world's leading credit bureaus. As I shared more about Co-owned with Dann, he shared more about how his life lessons embody many of the principles we aim to scale through Co-owned.

I have included his story below, as it was emblematic of the many stories shared by people I spoke to about Co-owned.

When you reflect on your life, there are always events and situations that impact your thoughts and thinking, particularly about money, and ultimately shape your future. For me, the first time I was ever introduced to saving and investing was actually by my grandfather, who bought me one share in Disney back in the early 1960s. One share of stock. This wasn't just any share of stock; this was Disney. I first visited Disneyland in 1963 and then later Disneyworld with my grandfather, who moved to Orlando in the 1970s. As word spread that Disney would be opening a theme park in his backyard, he made the decision to spare me another present of clothes or toys and gave me a Disney share. At the time, I asked him, 'So, does it get me into Disney?' He said, 'No, you are now an owner of the Disney World company and the magic it provides.' I didn't think too much about it but my mom would often remind me my Disney share was now worth X, or I now had two shares, then four and then eight as the company split over time. By the time I entered college, one share that cost approximately $25 at purchase was worth more than $1,000! Of course, I did what most college kids would do and sold half for spending money. Looking back, that decision cost me thousands and thousands of dollars!

Although Disney went public in 1957 at $13.88 a share, they split two-for-one three times before 1972 and then did a series of four-for-one and three-for-one splits. Bottom line: if you invested just $50 in 1957 (about four shares), you would now have close to 1,400 shares worth $140,000 today. I saw a Motley Fool analysis of this and they used a

$500 investment on IPO, which is now worth $1.4 million. The magic of compounding shares and dividends over a long period of time was indeed magic. Any other share of stock may not have made such an impact on me as a child but having a Disney share got my attention. Now, as a grandfather myself, one who now takes his grandchildren on annual Disney trips and cruises, you can bet I'm paying my grandfather's wisdom forward.

Peter Lynch, who managed Fidelity Investments and wrote the book One Up on Wall Street (1989) had a famous line: 'Invest in what you know.' He also backed it up with a stellar track record managing Magellan Funds with 29 per cent annual returns in the 1980s. We should consider 'buy what your kids know', which may be an even better mantra. The idea is not just the upside on the investment, it's the teaching opportunity that comes with explaining what a stock share is!

Anyone who has ever taken their kids to Build a Bear or watches Nickelodeon or Cartoon Network may want to pick up a share of Comcast, which is exactly what my granddaughter wanted to buy when I asked her if she would like to own part of this TV programme! She does now. The list of opportunities is endless: a share of Levi Strauss, Wendy's, Facebook (now Meta) or the early adopters to online gaming. The important point is that you can learn and earn – a great way to introduce saving for ownership in a company you love and use. The same concept can be applied at any age, with young adults or even mid-career. We tell consumers to save but we never teach them how to invest and the impact it can make over a lifetime.

So far, we have looked at the concepts behind co-owned. The next two chapters go on a deep dive into the economics, for both companies and consumers.

5

The economic case for companies

No one has ever become poor by giving.
— Anne Frank

C o-owned companies reward their customers with shares as they spend, which over time results in customer shareholders owning at least 10 per cent of the company. There isn't much science behind the 10 per cent, other than it feeling like a material enough number at which a company could reasonably be considered customer co-owned. Below 10 per cent feels like more of a marketing gimmick as opposed to embracing the model.

Earlier chapters of this book focused on the economic context and societal benefits for co-owned. In practice, co-owned will only be proactively adopted by companies at scale if it's adding value to existing company shareholders. As I wrote earlier, ESG or CSR initiatives rarely (if ever) get approved at the expense of shareholders. This chapter and those that follow provide a deep dive into the economic benefits for companies and their shareholders.

Today, co-owned is a big idea – but it's not yet a proven model. However, I believe there are enough data points to make a strong case for why it will work. This chapter, and indeed this book, is about setting out these data points and supporting arguments for executives and shareholders to consider in the context of their business.

Importantly, I'm not expecting any companies to give away 10 per cent of their value to their customers overnight. Instead, I'm proposing that companies embrace the co-owned concept, run tests with small but statistically significant samples of customers, assess what happens when customers are offered shares as they spend, and identify the potential value and optimal co-owned model for the company. The optimal model is one that adds value for both the company and its customers. And once the optimal model is found, companies will naturally want to scale it up, with customers owning at least 10 per cent of the company over time.

When I was first setting up Salary Finance, where I was seeking to convince large companies of the benefits to them (and their employees) of companies supporting the financial wellness of their employees, the most common question I got was, 'If it's such a good idea, why has nobody done it before?' I expect the same to happen with co-owned, where, similarly, I'm seeking to convince large companies of the benefits to them (and their customers) of focusing on the financial wellness of their customers. The answer, in my opinion, is that truly game-changing ideas rarely have perfect data at the start. It's more about the fundamentals. In this chapter and the next, you won't find exact data on the co-owned model but you will find compelling research and data that supports my argument, pointing to a conclusion that co-owned is a win–win model well worth testing. It goes without saying that, when it comes to innovation, the biggest gains are typically for companies that move quickly and learn fast.

Economic benefits of rewarding customers with shares

Issuing shares to customers as loyalty rewards offers a multitude of economic benefits to existing shareholders. Customer shareholders are more likely to be loyal, spend more with the company, refer friends and family and provide valuable insights, with the alignment in interests creating a win–win. In addition, customers can collectively provide an alternative and stable source of capital alongside institutional investors. Let's look at the benefits in turn.

Enhanced customer loyalty
(and less customer churn)

By rewarding customers with shares, companies create a sense of ownership among their customer base, which in turn drives loyalty. Shareholders typically have a deeper connection with a company if they have a stake in its success. Enhanced loyalty can lead to increased customer retention rates and higher customer lifetime value, which in turn boosts revenue and profitability. Furthermore, customers turned shareholders can become brand advocates, promoting the company's products or services and attracting new customers, further expanding the customer and shareholder base.

Increased share of wallet
(higher customer spend)

When customers become shareholders, they're likely to be more engaged with the company's offerings. They may increase their spending or frequency of purchases to support the company, with the company receiving more share of wallet in its respective category. This can result in a revenue boost for the company, benefiting all shareholders. Additionally, customer shareholders may be more willing to participate in upsell or cross-sell opportunities, driving additional sales and revenue growth.

Expanded market share
(higher customer numbers)

The promotion of issuing shares as rewards can also attract new customers to the company. The value proposition of becoming a shareholder through purchases or engagement programmes can differentiate the company from its competitors and attract a broader audience. As a result, the company's market reach can expand, leading to increased sales and market share. The growth in the customer base directly benefits existing shareholders, as the company's valuation and stock price can increase due to higher demand.

Access to customer insights

Customers turned shareholders can provide a valuable source of feedback and insights to the company. They have first-hand experience of the company's products or services and can offer valuable suggestions for improvement or innovation. By leveraging this customer feedback, the company can enhance its offerings, improve customer satisfaction and stay ahead of competitors. These improvements can lead to increased market share and profitability, benefiting all shareholders. The quality of feedback is likely to be much richer from customer shareholders than more traditional customer feedback requests, as customer shareholders have a more direct stake in the outcome.

Long-term stability and confidence

When customers become shareholders, they have a vested interest in the company's long-term success. They may be more likely to remain invested during periods of market volatility or economic uncertainty, providing stability to the shareholder base. This stability can result in reduced stock price volatility and increased investor confidence, attracting additional institutional and retail investors. A diverse and stable shareholder base contributes to a more robust market position for the company with the potential to further enhance shareholder value.

Results from a study by Columbia Business School

Columbia Business School is a leading business school in the US. In February 2021, it published a research paper called 'The effect of stock ownership on individual spending and loyalty' (Medina et al 2021). Following the study, it concluded that customers increase their spending at brands (companies) that issued shares as a reward.

One of the authors, Michaela Pagel, an associate professor of business at Columbia Business School, wrote: 'Our study is the first to show a very clean, causal link between stock ownership and consumption. It's not only that loyalty matters in people's investment decisions, but we show one step further that loyalty actually affects consumption of the very brands people are investing in.' (Columbia Business School 2021)

Broad findings

The researchers used transaction-level data from Bumped, an app that opened a share account for its users and rewarded them with shares from the brands they selected and ordinarily bought from. According to the study's press release, 'The researchers found that weekly spending at those brands jumped by 40 per cent after people received their brokerage accounts.' The researchers also studied a share grant programme that provided users with $5 or $10 share grants from the following companies: Red Robin, Taco Bell, McDonald's, Exxon Mobil, Chevron and Yum! Brands. The researchers found that, when users were granted a certain company's share(s), their weekly spending at those brands increased by 100 per cent – ie it doubled.

In terms of the psychological mechanisms at play, the study found that familiarity and loyalty heavily influence stockholders' spending decisions. Specifically, through survey evidence and data, 'loyalty appears to be the dominant psychological driver to higher spending'.

Pagel added, 'Investing is not just about maximising your returns, but people's preferences play a role. People buy brands they care about and we find that there's a direct link between spending and stock holdings.'

More detailed findings

The findings of the research have profound implications. As an independent and well-respected academic institution, Columbia Business School agrees with one of the central beliefs of co-owned: that share ownership increases customer loyalty and engagement. Given its importance, I've shared more detail from the report below. The methodology is one that can be used by companies to test the co-owned model for their own customers.

Scope

The study analysed transaction-level data as a part of a loyalty programme test that rewarded users with shares from brands they ordinarily buy from in the US. Customers signed up for a share reward account and linked all of their current, savings and credit card accounts. In turn, customers could select brands in several retail categories, and if and when they spent money on their selected brand(s), they received stock (shares) from that company.

Primary test – issuing stock in line with spending

The primary test assessed if rewarding consumers with shares as they spend, in brands they ordinarily buy from, leads to an increase in spending (share of wallet) at those companies.

Secondary test – issuing a one-time stock grant

The secondary test was a one-time stock grant of $5 or $10 in Red Robin, Taco Bell, McDonald's, Exxon Mobil, Chevron and Yum! Brands at the time of opening the rewards account, and then assessing the spending with those companies.

Efficacy safeguard

The study was designed to address the risk that individuals could time their sign-up to receive share rewards when they expect to make a lot of transactions. To address this, individuals in the sample were first required to sign up to a waiting list and remain there for an unknown period before getting their account, with no information given on how long the waiting list was. Users typically spent 4.5 months on the waiting list to ensure this efficacy risk was addressed. When users were invited to open their account, users in the study were only included if they opened their account within one week of being invited.

Dataset

There were 11,424 users in the study; 871 users were under 25, 9,431 between 25 and 49 and 1,122 over 50. Users were from across the US, with 67 per cent of users being male, 17 per cent female and 16 per cent not reporting. The study used daily data on each user's spending transactions from all linked current, savings and credit card accounts. For each linked account the study also used the corresponding history of transactions before and after each account was linked. It then flagged which brands were selected by users and as a result the transactions that were eligible for share rewards and whether they were actually rewarded.

The rewards programme test was launched in 2017 and transaction data for the study included the period from

2016 to 2020, so this data could be assessed before and after joining the reward programme. Overall, 11,424 users in the study were put on the waiting list and then received their rewards account. The users on average performed 730 transactions with an average of 2.4 cards being linked to the rewards programme. The average monthly total spending was $1,496 and the average total rewards were $37. Comparing the sample transaction data to the US Bureau of Labor Statistics Consumer Expenditure Survey showed that the spending levels of users were broadly similar to those of the US population (the average American spends $2,205 in a month and the shortfall was attributed to the study only including spending on 551 selected brands being tracked).

The secondary promotional programme described above was tested from March 2018. Users were automatically granted share(s) in the selected brands upon signing up for their rewards account. Users didn't know about the promotion at the time they signed up for the waitlist and only received the promotion if they'd spent money in those brands in their linked account's available transaction history. The grant was displayed with a description noting it was a 'thank you' for choosing the brand; 1,371 users were awarded grants during or one week after the week of opening an account.

Results

Figure 25 shows the raw data for eligible spending (brands that received a stock reward) and ineligible spending (brands that didn't receive a stock reward) eight weeks before and after account opening. The axis shows the percentage deviation of spending relative to the sample average in the eight weeks before and after account opening.

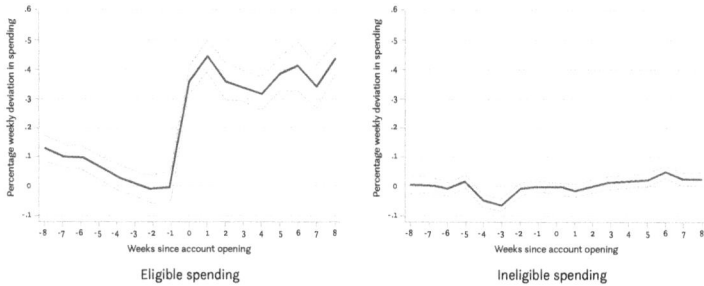

Eligible spending   Ineligible spending

Figure 25: This shows the percentage weekly deviation in spending, eight weeks before and after receiving the Bumped account, in the study and control groups (the dotted lines show the standard margin of error)

You can clearly see in the raw data that eligible spending (for brands where stock is provided) increased dramatically in the week of opening an account and stayed high for the full eight-week sample period. Conversely, there was no such rise where there were no stock rewards provided. In terms of US dollars, eligible spending averaged $56 per week, which corresponded approximately to a $22 increase in spending per week. Additionally, there wasn't a comparable pattern in ineligible spending. For the secondary test, eligible spending at the brands for which users received a grant increased even more, by about 100 per cent.

The study also looked at the eligible and ineligible spending beyond the eight-week sample period, up to six months. It concluded that there was still a significant increase in eligible spending. After the initial jump of 40 per cent, weekly spending stayed persistently high during the six-month review period. Finally, the study concluded that daily and weekly spending in certain brands for the user population is correlated with holdings of that company's stock.

Psychological hypotheses

The main point proven by the study's authors is that stock rewards alter customers' behaviours in ways that benefit the company. A section in the study on the psychological mechanisms pulls out some relevant conclusions from related research papers. If individuals perceive the rewards as a gift from the company from which they routinely purchase, they may feel the need to reciprocate by buying more from that company (Kube et al 2012). A reward in the form of shares is also likely to positively influence their consumption decisions (Li & Petrick 2008).

Receiving the shares of a certain company may make individuals believe that their actions are able to affect the company's stock price. (The study details the ample evidence that individuals tend to overestimate the likelihood of small probability events and their ability to influence them even if this isn't the case.)

The study suggests that customer shareholders could change their behaviour in a way that's favourable for the company (eg by avoiding buying substitute products from a competitor). The authors also note: 'Upon receiving shares, we expect customers to feel as part of a community and to perceive it as a betrayal if they engage in behaviour that can damage the company.'

The functioning of the rewards programme closely resembles the compensation programmes that engage executives through stocks (ie employee stock option programmes). The study provides evidence from these that the granting of shares leads to an increase in employee retention rates and that employee stock ownership plans increase productivity. Likewise, loyalty programmes align the incentives of executives and customers, who all benefit from a good performance of the firm. Furthermore, upon receiving shares, customers have an opportunity cost of not maintaining their affiliation with the company.

Summary

To recap, the researchers quantified the effects of awarding shares in certain companies on spending with those companies. With a statistically significant sample and a population sample that spends in line with the average American, it shows that weekly spending jumped 40 per cent and remained persistently high for at least six months (the study period) where stock was issued as a reward in line with spending, and a 100 per cent increase in spending in brands where stock was issued that wasn't directly linked to new spend. In addition to documenting a clean and causal link between stock ownership and spending, the research also showed that daily and weekly spending in certain brands was strongly correlated with holdings of that company's stock.

In a world where companies spend enormous amounts on marketing to stimulate growth and increase share of wallet from new and existing customers, the results from this study are compelling.

6

The cost to public companies of becoming co-owned

The previous chapter set out the potential gains of becoming customer co-owned. Now I will set out the potential costs, using two public companies as theoretical case studies, and demonstrate how those costs can be absorbed.

Example 1: BT

Company overview

BT is a major telecommunications company headquartered in the UK and listed on the FTSE 100. The business was originally founded in 1846 and has evolved to become a modern-day telecommunications giant. The company has invested significantly in innovation and driven advancements in areas such as full fibre and 5G connectivity. BT employs around 99,000 people (BT 2023).

Financials

In the year ending March 2023, BT delivered £20.7 billion in revenue and £1.9 billion in profit after tax. At the time of writing (May 2024), there are almost ten billion BT shares in circulation and each share has a share price of £1.06, creating an enterprise value of nearly £11 billion. The largest shareholder is Patrick Drahi, who owns 25 per cent of shares (2.4 million shares). According to Wikipedia, Drahi is an Israeli billionaire, telecoms businessman, media tycoon and investor. A former French citizen, he has been living in Switzerland since 1999. The other largest shareholders include T-Mobile (which owns 12 per cent of shares and is majority owned by German telecommunications company Deutsche Telekom) and institutional investors BNP Paribas (11 per cent), Blackrock (5 per cent), Schroder Investment Management (2 per cent), Vanguard (2 per cent) and Threadneedle Asset Management (2 per cent) (data from uk.marketscreener.com).

If you take the profit after tax and divide it by the number of shares in circulation, that gives earnings (ie profit) per share of around £0.19. Each BT share for the year ending March 2023 also earned a dividend of £0.08.

What's the cost to BT shareholders of being co-owned?

If BT shareholders chose to create new ordinary shares and issue them to customers so that they could become customer co-owned (for all of the reasons set out in earlier chapters), then around one billion new shares would need to be issued to customers for 10 per cent customer ownership. The face value of an ordinary share for BT is £0.05 (5p), which is the minimum price a new share can be issued at. If BT issued new shares to customers at this minimum price, the direct cost of issuing the new shares to customers for a 10 per cent customer ownership would therefore be £50 million.

Issuing new shares could also impact the share price, which would change the value of the shareholding of existing shareholders. While there are many factors to consider, arguably the worst-case scenario is a 10 per cent reduction in value for existing shareholders – the value transferred to customers. In practice this may be lower, as BT being co-owned could stimulate more demand for shares driven by an expectation of higher growth and profitability in future as a customer co-owned company.

If we plan for the worst-case scenario, after share issuance, earnings (ie profit) per share would reduce to £0.17 (from £0.19) as there are 10 per cent more shares for earnings (profit after tax) to be spread across. Similarly, the value of each share would reduce to £0.95 (from £1.06), as the same enterprise value is now split over 10 per cent more shares. Overall, £1.1 billion in enterprise value would transfer from existing shareholders to new customer shareholders, with an incremental £209 million in profit after tax needing to be created to maintain the same earnings per share across the larger share pool and as a result maintain the same share price (all other things being equal).

How can the cost be recovered so that being co-owned accretes value for existing BT shareholders?

Summarising the above, there are two costs to BT and its existing shareholders. First, the £50 million cost of issuing new ordinary shares to customers; and second, the incremental £209 million profit after tax required to maintain the same earnings per share across the larger share pool (including 10 per cent new customer shares) and as a result maintain the share price and share value for existing shareholders (all other things being equal).

Note that BT has 14 million household customers in the UK. Simplistically, dividing profit after tax by each household creates a current profit after tax per household of £136. In practice it's lower, as BT also has business clients and overseas revenue streams, but this is a helpful reference metric.

The £50 million one-off cost of issuing ordinary shares (5p each) could reasonably be covered by customer shareholders receiving the reward shares, so it wouldn't be a cost for BT or existing shareholders. For each share, customer shareholders would pay 5p and receive a share worth £1.06, so this is a very fair trade. In aggregate, the 10 per cent of new ordinary shares issued to customers would be worth £1.1 billion or £76 for each BT customer household; taking off the 5p cost of the ordinary share issuance would make the value £72 to each customer household. In addition, each customer, through dividends, based on the year ending March 2023, would receive £5.50 in annual dividend.

There are multiple ways in which the £209 million in incremental profit after tax can be delivered to maintain the same earnings per share. Illustratively, 50 per cent (£105 million) could be covered by switching existing marketing and sales spend and 50 per cent through increased customer profitability. These are expanded below.

In the year ending March 2023, BT spent £952 million on marketing, sales and sales commissions. Fifty per cent of the incremental profit requirement (£105 million) amounts to a 11 per cent saving in marketing and sales costs (by switching, ie using marketing budget to pay for shares issued to customers). This seems reasonable as, if executed well, being co-owned should replace the need for a sizeable marketing budget. In addition, delivering the remaining £105 million from incremental profit per customer household amounts to £7.50 per customer household (incremental 5.5 per cent), which again seems reasonable given that customer shareholders are more likely to be loyal (reducing the 1 per cent churn per month currently estimated for BT retail customers). Customer shareholders could increase referrals to family and friends, share valuable new customer insights and be more open to cross-sell and upsell opportunities. This would also attract new customers to the co-ownership opportunity. It would only require a tiny fraction of the 40 per cent growth in spend set out in the Columbia Business School study to be cost neutral but with the potential for it to be hugely value accretive.

Unit economics

As set out earlier in the chapter, no big company is expected to issue 10 per cent of their shares to their customers overnight. Instead, the expectation is that they will select small cohorts of customers and test the economic impact of issuing shares as rewards. Once the economics are proven with a win–win co-owned model, it can be gradually rolled out and scaled up.

At an individual customer level, for BT, the economic test is a relatively simple one. If an example retail customer spends, say, £300 per year (£25 per month on their phone line) and they're issued shares in the year worth 3 per cent of spend (£9), does the impact of this £9 of share spend by BT generate more than £9 of earnings (profit) for BT? This could be from the customer reducing the probability of churn, switching their other products to BT (eg broadband), referring family and friends or taking part in customer feedback surveys. Each action could be rewarded with loyalty points that convert to shares.

Summary

Given the critical infrastructure it provides, BT is an organisation that commands significant national interest. It's currently more than 50 per cent owned by four institutional investors. This institutional investor concentration risks volatility in share price and governance, which doesn't represent public opinion in a way that matches the level of national interest. The addition of customer co-shareholders, as well as being value accretive for shareholders and customers, has the potential to add governance that better represents society. The practicalities of including customers in shareholder governance are explored in Chapter 11.

Example 2: Tesco

Company overview

Tesco plc, listed on the FTSE 100, was founded in 1919 and is now the largest grocery retailer in the UK. It operates online and through retail stores, with 3,712 retail stores in the UK and 1,147 retail stores in the Republic of Ireland, Czech Republic, Slovakia and Hungary. The Tesco Group also includes: Tesco Bank, Tesco Mobile, a network of One Stop convenience stores, Booker (a wholesale business) and dunnhumby, a data science business. The group employs around 330,000 people (Tesco 2023).

Tesco has a 27.3 per cent market share. The retail grocery market was, until recently, dominated by the 'big four' supermarkets: Tesco, Sainsbury's, Asda and Morrisons. In response to rises in the cost of living, consumer demand is shifting in favour of lower-cost retailers such as Aldi and Lidl. In September 2022, Aldi took over fourth place in the grocery store ranking for the first time. A primary strategic focus for all supermarkets, including Tesco, is now delivering value for money.

After value for money, Tesco's second listed strategic priority is increasing loyalty, which it does through its well-developed loyalty rewards programme, Tesco Clubcard. The Clubcard enables a personalised shopping experience for customers by leveraging customer insights. It also enables incremental revenue opportunities with suppliers to help them offer customers tailored and relevant products. Tesco has 21 million active Clubcard households.

Financials

In the year ending March 2023, Tesco delivered £65.8 billion in revenue and £753 million in profit after tax. At the time of writing (May 2024), there are 7.4 billion Tesco shares in circulation and each share has a share price of £3.05, creating an enterprise value of £22.6 billion. Tesco is 78 per cent owned by institutional investors, 18 per cent by the general public and 3 per cent by employees (Simply Wall Street 2024). The largest institutional shareholders are Silchester International Investors (5 per cent), Schroder Investment Management Limited (5 per cent), Vanguard (3 per cent), FIL Investment Advisors (3 per cent), Norges Bank Investment Management (3 per cent) and Blackrock (3 per cent).

If you take the profit after tax and divide it by the number of shares in circulation, that gives earnings (ie profit) per share of £0.10. Each Tesco share for the year ending March 2023 earned a dividend of £0.11.

What's the cost to Tesco shareholders of being co-owned?

If Tesco shareholders chose to create new ordinary shares and issue them to customers so they became customer co-owned (for all of the reasons set out in earlier chapters), then around 740 million new shares would need to be issued to customers for 10 per cent customer ownership. The face value of an ordinary share for Tesco is £0.06, which is the minimum price a new share can be issued at. So the direct cost of issuing the new shares to customers at this minimum price, for a 10 per cent customer ownership, would be around £44 million.

Issuing new shares would have the same expected consequences as for BT. Again, if we plan for the worst-case scenario, then after share issuance, earnings per share would reduce to £0.09 (from £0.10), as there are 10 per cent more shares for earnings to be spread across. Similarly, the value of each share would reduce to £2.75 (from £3.05), as the same enterprise value is now split over 10 per cent more shares. In this second example, an incremental £83 million in profit after tax would need to be created to maintain the same earnings per share across the larger share pool.

How can the cost be recovered?

Again, there would be two costs to Tesco and its existing shareholders. First, the £44 million cost of issuing new ordinary shares to customers; and second, the incremental £83 million profit after tax required. Simplistically, dividing profit after tax by each Clubcard household creates a current profit after tax per household of £36. As with BT, the cost of issuing shares could reasonably be covered by customer shareholders receiving the reward shares, and there are multiple ways in which the £83 million in incremental profit after tax can be delivered to maintain the same earnings per share.

In this example, if a retail customer spends £1,800 per year with Tesco on their shopping and they're issued shares during the year worth 3 per cent of spend (£54), the impact of this £54 of share spend by Tesco can easily generate more than £54 of earnings. This could be from reducing other costs (for example, offering share rewards instead of other loyalty rewards) and increasing revenue through increased share of wallet (customers doing more of their shopping at Tesco instead of other supermarkets).

Summary

Tesco is the largest retailer in the UK but it faces significant headwinds as customers prioritise cost above all else. The way to counter this, in addition to providing good value (a prerequisite), is to build customer loyalty and increase share of wallet. Tesco has a good loyalty programme already through its Tesco Clubcard. Sainsbury's, the second-largest retailer, also has this with their Nectar programme. Issuing stock rewards as an additional benefit has the potential to drive incremental loyalty to maintain market leadership in an increasingly competitive market. Stock rewards is the next frontier in loyalty programmes.

Overall, for public companies in both the UK and US, the economics of issuing shares to customers are fundamentally the same. The minimum cost of issuing ordinary shares is typically marginal (usually a few pence or cents at most), which can be covered by customers who receive the full share price minus the cost of the ordinary share (for example, at the time of writing, Tesla has an ordinary share price of \$0.001 and a share price of around \$185). If executed well, a company being customer co-owned should be seen as a positive by investors and able to maintain or grow the share price after the customer share issuance. At worst, a 10 per cent share issuance to customers could reduce earnings per share and share value by 10 per cent, which would need to be covered by an incremental 11 per cent profit. This and more should be achievable through increased customer loyalty and engagement, core determinants of profit and value, as customers have a stake in the success of the company.

Of course, share price movements aren't an exact science. It's possible that companies issue new shares and increase earnings per share (EPS) in proportion, but the share price dilution of issuing new shares for existing shareholders remains (ie the increase in earnings doesn't increase the share price proportionally after the dilution of issuing new shares). In which case, companies could also consider a share buyback (instead of issuing new shares), using the incremental earnings from being customer co-owned to fund the share buyback for customers. In practice, customers and investors in every company will react differently and the key is for companies to test the model on a small set of customers and to assess the impact, just as Columbia Business School did in its research report.

7

The economics for private equity-owned companies

As set out in Chapter 3, alongside public companies, trillions of pounds' worth of companies are owned by private equity firms in the UK and US, including many leading consumer brands. In the UK, nearly £80 billion has been spent by private equity firms taking public companies private in the past five years alone (Louch & Levingston 2023). Private equity-owned companies in the UK include Morrisons, Asda and John Laing, and in the US Staples and Dollar General. Private equity firms and financial investors have also become active in buying sports teams. Recent examples include Eldridge Industries (founded by Todd Boehly), which acquired Chelsea Football Club in the UK. They also co-own the LA Dodgers and LA Sparks in the US. Fenway Sports Group owns Liverpool Football Club in the UK and Boston Red Sox in the US.

In this chapter, I will set out a summary of how the private equity industry works and how the co-owned model can be applied within it, creating economic value for all parties. The private equity pathway is now well trodden, with a well-defined process. Private equity firms pool together substantial capital from private (family office) and institutional (including pension funds and endowments) investors to form investment funds. They then carefully target businesses with untapped value in the form of growth potential and/or operational inefficiencies. Through due diligence, financial analysis and negotiation, the private equity firm acquires a controlling stake in the target business. Once acquired, the private equity firm initiates a value creation phase, partnering with its selected management team and leveraging its expertise, networks and operational capabilities to drive growth and enhance profitability. This involves implementing strategic initiatives, operational improvements and cost optimisation measures to unlock the target company's value potential. The ultimate goal is to exit the investment at a substantial profit, typically after a period of three to seven years. The exit options can vary and may include initial public offerings (IPOs), secondary market sales or trade sales to strategic buyers. Private equity firms seek to maximise the value of their investment by carefully timing the exit to capture the full potential of the target company's growth trajectory.

On the face of it, private equity has its benefits. It invests in the growth of private companies and in doing so creates a substantial return for its shareholders (including, for example, pension funds, which serve an important role in funding the retirement of an increasingly elderly population) and, of course, the executives of the private equity firm and acquired company (quasi-shareholders). However, these benefits are traded against a set of unfavourable outcomes which are commonly bestowed on the industry. These are summarised below.

Job losses: Private equity value enhancement typically involves material cost-cutting measures, which often means job losses.

Short-term focus: They're typically focused on a short time horizon of between three to seven years to create value. This short-term focus can lead to a prioritisation of quick financial gains over long-term strategic planning. Companies may be pressured to prioritise short-term profitability, potentially at the expense of long-term growth, research and development or sustainable business practices.

Excessive leverage: Private equity transactions often involve significant amounts of debt to finance acquisitions. The use of leverage can amplify returns when investments perform well but it also increases risks. In some cases, if the company's performance weakens or market conditions change (such as rising interest rates to service the debt), excessive debt burdens can lead to financial distress or bankruptcy.

Lack of transparency: Private equity operates in a relatively opaque manner compared to public companies. Limited disclosure requirements mean that investors and the public may have limited visibility into the operations, financial performance and governance practices of private equity-owned companies. This lack of transparency can raise concerns about accountability and may hinder the assessment of potential risks or conflicts of interest.

Financial engineering: Private equity firms often employ various financial strategies to enhance returns, such as leveraged buyouts, dividend recapitalisations and asset stripping. While these tactics can generate short-term gains for investors, they can also burden companies with excessive debt or drain their resources, potentially weakening the long-term viability of the business.

Lack of stakeholder alignment: Private equity firms primarily aim to maximise returns for their investors. This focus may create a misalignment of interests with other stakeholders such as employees, customers, suppliers and local communities. Decisions made by private equity owners, including layoffs, plant closures or outsourcing, may prioritise investor returns at the expense of these other stakeholders.

Regulatory concerns: Some critics argue that the private equity industry is subject to less regulation and oversight compared to public companies. This lighter regulatory framework can raise concerns about potential abuses, conflicts of interest or inadequate protections for employees, investors or the broader economy.

Overall, in practice, there are both positives and negatives to the private equity industry. The positives arguably outweigh the negatives, with investment fundamentally driving growth, which in turn drives opportunity. However, private equity represents a good example of the polarisation of society between shareholders (private equity being the ultimate beneficiaries) and the common person. Rather than pitting each side against the other, rather than an ongoing debate about who is right or more virtuous, we should put both on the same side through co-owned.

In the context of a private equity transaction, the owners would issue shares to customers that account for at least 10 per cent of the company. In doing so, customers, alongside the owners, both stand to benefit after the typical three- to seven-year hold period. As set out above, incentivising customers through shares leads to an alignment in interests, which drives loyalty and engagement, which drives value for the company. In this model, private equity shareholders are rewarded for the deployment of their capital, risk taking and delivering their value enhancement plan, and customer shareholders are rewarded for their loyalty and engagement, which similarly helps to increase the value of the company. The private equity firm should see an increase in the value of its exit at least proportional, likely more, than its customer share issuance, so is likely better off, creating a win–win.

Socially, this will also help to reduce public hostility towards increasing private equity ownership of well-known brands. In relation to sports clubs, fans underpin the value of those clubs; without them a sports team is economically defunct. Aligning the interests of fans with the private equity firm could go a long way towards creating less unrest and allowing everyone to focus on creating and supporting a winning team and the underlying business.

8

Next-generation loyalty programmes

My previous company, Salary Finance, was based on a big idea and implemented through the well-established channel of an employee benefit programme. Similarly, Co-owned is a big idea, which will be implemented through the well-established channel of a customer loyalty programme. Co-owned is well positioned to spearhead the next generation of customer loyalty programmes. These programmes are more popular with consumers than ever, having improved significantly in recent years with enhanced personalisation, digital offerings, 'gamification' (elements of gameplay or challenges) and paywalls (subscription programmes). In this chapter, I will summarise some of the key industry research to help understand this industry segment and how Co-owned can fit into it. The statistics are largely US based but the fundamentals apply just as much in the UK.

In the US, more than 90 per cent of companies now have some form of loyalty programme (Wollan et al 2017). This is driven by 65 per cent of a company's revenue typically coming from the repeat business of existing customers (Miller 2022), it being 5 to 25 times more expensive to acquire a new customer than to keep an existing one (Gallo 2014). It has been found that 57 per cent of consumers spend more on brands or providers to which they are loyal (Wollan et al 2017), and a 5 per cent increase in customer retention correlates with a 25 per cent increase in profit (Reichheld 2001). All of this results in a customer loyalty management market that's valued at more than $5.5 billion (in the US only), with the market expected to surpass $24 billion by the end of 2028 (Faria 2023). Figure 26 below shows example industries where there's huge potential for future growth (I note that this is for paid subscription programmes but it's likely illustrative for free programmes as well).

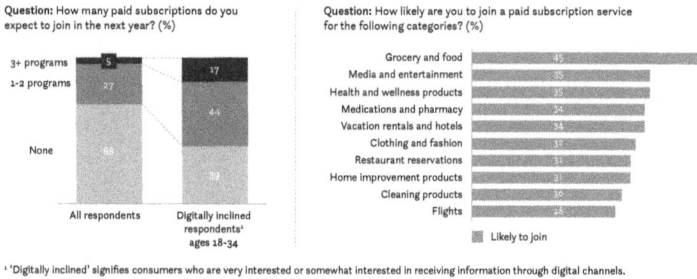

Question: How many paid subscriptions do you expect to join in the next year? (%)

	All respondents	Digitally inclined respondents[1] ages 18-34
3+ programs	5	17
1-2 programs	27	44
None	68	39

Question: How likely are you to join a paid subscription service for the following categories? (%)

Grocery and food	45
Media and entertainment	35
Health and wellness products	35
Medications and pharmacy	34
Vacation rentals and hotels	34
Clothing and fashion	13
Restaurant reservations	11
Home improvement products	11
Cleaning products	10
Flights	8

■ Likely to join

[1] 'Digitally inclined' signifies consumers who are very interested or somewhat interested in receiving information through digital channels.

Figure 26: Paid programmes show high potential for growth across several categories

Successful loyalty programmes generate meaningful top and bottom-line results for companies through customer loyalty and engagement. According to a report by Accenture (2016), members of US loyalty programmes generate 12–18 per cent more incremental revenue growth per year than non-members. Data analysis platform PYMNTS stated in a June 2024 report that 83 per cent of consumers say belonging to a loyalty programme influences their decision to buy again from a brand; while 75 per cent of consumers in loyalty programmes will buy more products from the companies they partner with (PYMNTS 2022); and a Neilsen survey in 2013 found that 84 per cent of consumers say they're more likely to visit retailers that offer a loyalty programme (BusinessWire 2013). As with most things, success is determined by the quality of the programme's design and execution. Figure 27 shows the difference in performance between the bottom- and top-performing programmes.

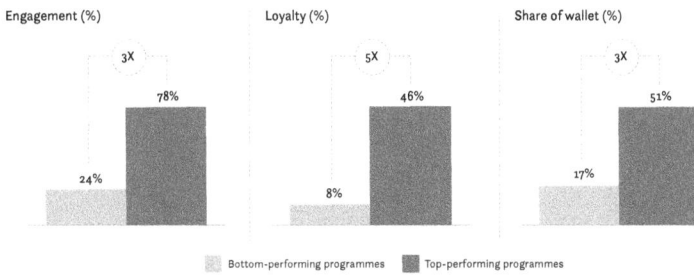

Figure 27: Top-performing programmes see higher engagement and loyalty, boosting spending

In 1995, *Harvard Business Review* reported that rewards programmes are widely misunderstood and often misapplied (O'Brien & Jones 1995). When it comes to design and implementation, they commented that too many companies treat rewards as short-term promotional giveaways or specials of the month. Approached that way, rewards can create some value by motivating new or existing customers to try a product or service – but until they're designed to build loyalty, they return at best a small fraction of their potential value.

A rewards programme can accelerate the loyalty life cycle, encouraging first- or second-year customers to behave like a company's most profitable tenth-year customers – but only if it's planned and implemented as part of a larger loyalty management strategy. A company must find ways to share value with customers in proportion to the value the customers' loyalty creates for the company. The goal must be to develop a system through which customers are continually educated about the rewards of loyalty and motivated to earn them. Achieving sustainable loyalty, measured in years, requires a sustainable strategic approach.

An analysis by Boston Consulting Group (Hearne et al 2023) says, 'Loyalty programmes should be designed with focused objectives in line with the company's overall strategy. Is the main objective to increase customer engagement and loyalty? To add new revenue streams or increase share of the customer wallet? Is it to increase purchasing frequency or average basket size, or both?' A loyalty programme can be used to reach a variety of objectives, using different tools accordingly.

While being co-owned and offering share rewards is a simple concept, there are many important design decisions that will determine success. Hearne et al suggest businesses should ask the following questions:

- How should our market position and long-term strategy shape the vision and objectives for the loyalty programme?
- Which customers are we designing for? Existing or potential? Particular income levels or age groups?
- What will truly affect their behaviour?
- How can we use the programme to differentiate ourselves?
- How does our perceived product value shape the benefits we should offer?
- Is the design going to be durable over time as customer behaviour changes?
- What tangible benefits can we give customers that provide the highest value at the lowest relative cost?

In recent years, several consumer-facing brands have been experimenting with new programme models, including community engagement. For example, beauty brand Sephora has built a community through in-store workshops and wellness and beauty events. The 34 million customers registered for its Beauty Insider Community can engage with one another by seeking advice, taking part in challenges, sharing tips and posting photos (Feger 2023). Communities like this can reinforce an emotional connection with a brand and promote loyalty.

This concept can be applied to a co-owner community to create deeper connections and brand advocates within the customer shareholder community. Creating an engaged loyalty programme has many benefits. According to PYMNTS (2022), six out of ten consumers involved in US loyalty programmes have more positive experiences with these brands because they believe their connection transcends the transactional. In a 2021 global consumer survey, Yotpo found that 56 per cent of consumers are willing to spend more with a brand they like even if cheaper options exist (Polkes 2020). Salesforce reported that 95 per cent of customers say trusting a company increases their loyalty (Otis Leder 2019); and Accenture found that 14 per cent of the most loyal customers express their loyalty by publicly endorsing or defending a company via social media (Wollan et al 2017). Increasingly, we live in a world driven by values, with 63 per cent of respondents surveyed for The Loyalty Report 2022 agreeing that they're more likely to do business with brands/companies whose purpose aligns with their values (Bond Brand Loyalty 2022). While popular culture tends to idolise high net worth individuals and companies that make a lot of profit, the tide is turning to idolising people and companies who do good for others.

These statistics aren't lost on the industry. According to Antavo's 2022 North America Customer Loyalty Report, 80 per cent of loyalty programme owners were likely or very likely to revamp their loyalty programme in the next three years and to increase or significantly increase their investments in customer loyalty. Similarly, 87.5 per cent of loyalty programme owners planned to engage with customers in non-transactional ways in the next three years (Antavo 2022).

Recent success stories include Amazon Prime members spending more than double that of non-member Amazon customers (Green 2018); Walmart+ members spending an average of $79 per online visit, compared to $62 for non-members (Repko 2022); Walmart+ members shopping an average of 11 more times per year (29 visits) compared with non-members (18); and Adidas adiClub members buying 50 per cent more often than non-members (Johnston 2022). Adidas adiClub members' lifetime value is double that of non-members, and American Airlines' AAdvantage loyalty programme is worth tens of billions of dollars – more than double the valuation of the airline (Ross-Smith 2022). Co-owned has the potential to be the next frontier in customer loyalty programmes.

Some companies are already starting to experiment with new kinds of perks for retail customer share-holders, demonstrating the scope for innovation in loyalty programmes. The international cruise line Carnival, for example, offers onboard credit for travellers who own more than £1,000 of its shares – this is helping the company to recover from the impact of the Covid-19 pandemic on travel and at a time when dividends have not been possible.

Meanwhile anyone with at least 64 shares in Whitbread can benefit from free breakfasts at Premier Inn hotels and 10 per cent off at restaurants owned by the group. And all shareholders of Legal & General qualify for discounts and rewards across its insurance and other financial products (Nathan 2024). Going a step further with a co-owned model would provide all manner of opportunities to expand loyalty offerings of this kind.

Conclusion

Over recent decades, company shareholders have been capitalism's big winners. Unintentionally, this has been at the expense of the common person. How long can this continue? There are likely two paths ahead, just as in the 1920/30s – authoritarianism or taxation. Neither is good for companies and their shareholders. Rather than fighting the shareholder capitalism paradigm, we should make capitalism more inclusive and align incentives to create shareholder wealth for everyone.

Naturally, there will be a first-mover advantage for companies that act first and fast and implement the co-owned model in the most thoughtful and effective way. While not all company executives and shareholders will want to acknowledge that capitalism is broken (because it's working well for them), the beauty of co-owned is that they don't have to: the customer loyalty dimension makes it an economically rational thing to do.

Salary Finance was ultimately about improving the financial health of workers. While many companies questioned whether this was their role (and commonly called us 'paternalistic'), they understood the broader employee benefits market that Salary Finance could neatly fit into and adopted it as part of their employee benefits strategy. Sometimes profound change can happen through simple actions and extensions to existing initiatives. In this way, Co-owned can dovetail perfectly with the well-established and rapidly growing customer loyalty market.

9

The economic case for consumers

An investment in knowledge pays the best interest.
— attributed to Benjamin Franklin

The previous chapter set out the economic case for companies to become co-owned. This chapter looks at the co-ownership model from the consumer's perspective. Clearly, the proposition needs to be compelling for both parties. The key question is, can co-owned really make a meaningful difference in the lives of consumers and be the catalyst for addressing the mass impoverishment of the common person? I believe so, and this section sets out both the direct and indirect benefits.

Direct benefits

In Chapter 11, I'll look at different ways in which companies can implement the co-owned model. For the purposes of this chapter, I'll investigate the financial benefits to customers using a simple illustrative co-owned model: (a) companies reward their customers with shares worth 3 per cent of each purchase; and (b) customers round up each purchase by 10 per cent to buy additional shares (the practicalities of how this can be done will be covered in Chapter 11).

Methodology

To illustrate the financial benefits to the average customer in this co-owned model, the following methodology was used. I started by taking the Office of National Statistics (ONS) data on average household spend by spend category over the past ten years in the UK (ONS 2022). I then mapped each spend category to an example public company. For example, I mapped the spending on food and drinks to

Tesco (the UK's largest retailer) and then mapped water charges to Severn Trent (a public water company). I then calculated for each of the past ten years the cumulative share value of the co-owned model set out above: (a) companies providing a reward of shares worth 3 per cent of each purchase (eg each time a customer shops at Tesco they would be rewarded with shares worth 3 per cent of the purchase price); and (b) customers rounding up their purchases by 10 per cent, with that amount being used to buy further shares.

Headline results

According to the ONS survey, households in the UK spent on average £529 per week or £27,498 per year in 2022. Based on the ONS breakdown, I mapped 77 per cent of this spend to an example public company (explained below). Over the ten-year period from 2013 to 2023, if companies rewarded their customers with shares worth 3 per cent of each purchase and if customers bought shares equivalent to rounding up each purchase by 10 per cent, then the average customer today would have amassed £88,278 of share wealth. Of this, £29,159 is the amount of money customers would have invested as part of the 10 per cent round-up, and £59,119 is the reward share value and the cumulative share price gain in the period.

In a country where one in four adults has less than £100 in savings, clearly almost £90,000 of share wealth accumulation is transformational. All of this for two simple actions: one from public companies (the 3 per cent share reward) and one from customers (the 10 per cent round-up share purchase amount).

If you take this a step further and add in automatic share purchases for internet companies where consumers spend their time, then the share wealth creation becomes even greater. For example, adding in £1 investment in Meta (Facebook's parent company) for every 100 minutes spent on Facebook and a £0.30 share reward from Meta, plus a £0.10 investment in Alphabet (Google's parent) for every search on Google and a £0.03 share reward from Alphabet, this increases the wealth accumulated over ten years from £88,278 to £98,370 for the average UK household – a life-changing amount. The same fundamentals apply for the US. In Chapter 11 I'll cover how this can work for customers in a low-friction way, ie making it easy for consumers to buy shares as they spend.

More detailed analysis

If you're thinking that this all sounds too good to be true, it is. Not every public company is going to provide 3 per cent share rewards and not every consumer is going to round up their spending in public companies by 10 per cent to buy shares each time they shop, even though they arguably should (and that's not investment advice). But what this analysis shows is that the idea has meaningful potential.

The table and commentary overleaf set out the methodology used and the results.

(1) Household spend type	(2) Example matched public company	(3) % of annual household spend	(4) Yearly spend (in 2022)	(5) Cumulative Share value (£)	(6) Cumulative invested (£)	(7) Return made (£)
Food, drinks, other supermarket spend	Tesco	19%	£5,179	£10,394	£6,288	£4,106
Electronics, clothing, garden, pets	Amazon	11%	£3,135	£14,940	£3,806	£11,134
Water charges	Severn Trent	2%	£426	£928	£517	£411
Electricity and gas	SSE	5%	£1,405	£3,226	£1,529	£1,697
Household goods	Dunelm	7%	£1,903	£4,563	£2,310	£2,253
Household maintenance goods	B&M	1%	£355	£5,716	£3,942	£1,774
Vehicle purchase, repairs and servicing	Tesla	7%	£1,930	£37,929	£2,344	£35,586
Petrol, diesel and motor oils	Shell	4%	£982	£2,295	£1,192	£1,103
Airfares	BA	2%	£613	£590	£744	-£154
Communications	BT	4%	£1,012	£957	£1,229	-£271
Package holidays	TUI	2%	£547	£163	£541	-£379
Household, medical and life insurances	L&G	8%	£2,159	£4,212	£2,621	£1,592
Vehicle insurance	Direct Line	2%	£536	£560	£651	-£91
Mortgage payments	Barclays	4%	£1,191	£1,804	£1,446	£358
SUB-TOTAL		**77%**	£21,372	£88,278	£29,160	£59,119

(8) Internet time spend type						
Social	Facebook (Meta)			£4,622	£1,404	£3,217
Search	Google (Alphabet)			£5,470	£1,606	£3,864
SUB-TOTAL				£10,092	£3,010	£7,082
GRAND TOTAL				£98,370	£32,170	£66,200

Each of the numbered categories in the table is explained below.

(1) Household spend type. This column pulls out and groups spend items in the ONS household spend survey. It includes only spend items that could be reasonably mapped to a public company; in fact, 77 per cent of average household spend could reasonably be mapped to a public company. The remaining 33 per cent of household spend was in categories where there was no obvious linked public company, for example education fees.

(2) Example matched public company. This column maps the spend category to an example public company. I chose a large and well-known public company as an illustrative example. There was no particular science to which companies I selected in the category, other than choosing a large and well-known household brand. For 'food, drinks, other supermarket spend' I chose Tesco; I could equally have chosen Sainsbury's, the UK's second-largest food retailer and also a public company.

(3) Percentage of annual household spend. Based on ONS survey data in 2022, I calculated the percentage of annual household spend in that spend category relative to the overall household spend. I then took the total ONS survey household spend in each of the past ten years and, for simplicity, applied the same 2022 percentage spend in each category in each year.

(4) Yearly spend (in 2022). Based on the ONS data, I aggregated the spend (in GBP) in each spend category in 2022. Although not shown in the summary table, I estimated the spend in each category for each of the past ten years by taking the ONS total household spend figure in each year and again applying the same percentage as in 2022.

(5) Cumulative share value (£). Here I calculated the cumulative share value of the co-owned model. Between 2013 and 2023, I calculated how many shares would have been acquired each year, based on companies providing 3 per cent of spend in shares and consumers rounding up their spending by 10 per cent to buy additional shares and taking into account the growth (or decline) in share price, and the addition of dividends being reinvested. This represents the share value an average household would have today if this model had been adopted ten years ago. In aggregate, this comes to £88,278 and the breakdown by spend category and associated public company can be seen in the table.

(6) Cumulative invested (£). This shows how much of the share value today represents money (GBP) invested by consumers as part of the 10 per cent round-up. In aggregate, this comes to £29,160 and the breakdown by company can be seen in the table.

(7) Return made (£). This shows how much profit is made above the amount invested through the round-ups. In aggregate, this comes to £59,119 and the breakdown by company can be seen in the table. The level of gain is, of course, determined by the level of growth in the stock price over the years. Tesla has clearly performed well; indeed, companies that consumers are spending their money in today could do just as well in the next ten years.

(8) Internet time spend type. The first section of the table focuses on where consumers 'spend their money' and this part provides two examples of where consumers 'spend their time' and illustrates the benefits of investing in those areas also. Although internet giants such as Facebook already have vast amounts of data on customer behaviour, they face significant competition from alternative social networks (eg TikTok), and their high share prices require continued loyalty and growth to be justified. Hence I believe these businesses and their users would again benefit from a co-owned approach. With that in mind, I have included consumer investment in representative internet platforms as part of my analysis. (See also Chapter 11 on Twitter/X.)

It models the financial gains between 2013 and 2023 of adding in £1 investment in Meta for every 100 minutes spent on Facebook and a £0.30 share reward from Meta, plus £0.10 investment in Alphabet for every search on Google and a £0.03 share reward from Alphabet. This increases the wealth accumulated over ten years from £88,278 to £98,370 for the average household, based on average consumer usage of Facebook and Google.

Summary of direct benefits

The results speak for themselves. Investing little and often in the companies you spend your money and time in adds up, especially when companies provide share rewards and when taking into account share compound growth over multiple years. However, these benefits don't take into account the benefits of the co-owned model helping to increase the value of these companies through increased loyalty and engagement and speeding up innovation cycles through customer feedback.

Clearly there are a lot of assumptions at play here. And, of course, investment predictions are never precise. But what I took away from the analysis is that the collective gains are not marginal but transformational. In a country where one in four households has almost no savings, a £98,370 accumulation of share wealth for two simple actions would completely change the game in equality and mass impoverishment. Even 10 per cent of this would make a huge difference for many.

Financial education: an indirect benefit

As the quote at the start of this chapter says, 'An investment in knowledge pays the best interest'. As is widely reported, there's a lack of financial literacy among the general population, driven by a chronic lack of financial education. Young people enter the workplace without the necessary financial education or role models (including their parents) and typically 'learn by doing' and 'learn through mistakes'. The challenge of this approach for the common person with limited financial resources is that financial mistakes can be hard to recover from. Examples include: problem debt that impacts credit scores and access to credit (including mortgages) for years to come; a lack of budgeting skills, creating no room for savings or investments; and realising too late in life the importance of investing in a pension early to benefit from compound growth that will fund a dignified retirement.

Engaging customers as co-shareholders not only directly creates monetary value but it also creates the opportunity to engage customers in practical financial education, learning about how companies, shares and investments work as well as the general fundamentals of money management. As mentioned before, the practicalities of how this can be implemented will be covered in Chapter 11. The rest of this chapter looks at the benefits of increasing the financial education of the common person at an individual and societal level.

Through my work as chair of MyBnk (the UK's largest financial education charity for young people), I've witnessed the low levels of financial literacy in the UK and the challenges in addressing it at scale. I'll share some research on financial education to bring the opportunity and challenges to life as we consider how best to implement co-owned in a manner that also increases financial literacy.

The power of financial education for consumers: In an increasingly complex and interconnected financial world, the need for financial education among consumers has never been more critical. Empowering consumers with the knowledge and skills to make informed financial decisions is essential for their personal wellbeing and the overall stability of the economy. There's extensive research that supports the benefits of financial education for consumers and provides evidence for how financial education positively impacts individual financial behaviours, fosters economic resilience and contributes to a more financially inclusive society.

Improving financial literacy: At the heart of financial education lies the goal of improving financial literacy (see Mitchell & Lusardi 2011). This encompasses the knowledge, understanding and competence required to effectively manage personal finances. Numerous studies have consistently shown that a large segment of the population lacks basic financial knowledge, including concepts such as budgeting, saving and investing, and debt management (Hastings et al 2013). Financial education plays a pivotal role in addressing this knowledge gap.

Research by Lusardi & Mitchell (2014) demonstrates that financial literacy is positively associated with better financial decision making, increased savings and reduced debt levels. Consumers who receive financial education tend to exhibit improved awareness of financial products, increased confidence in their financial abilities and greater participation in long-term financial planning (Remund 2010). Consequently, as financial literacy improves, individuals are better equipped to make prudent financial choices, leading to enhanced financial and personal wellbeing.

Mitigating financial risks: The ability to identify and mitigate financial risks is a crucial skill for consumers, particularly in the face of economic uncertainty. Research suggests that financially educated individuals are more likely to engage in risk-reducing behaviours such as holding diversified investment portfolios and purchasing insurance (Van Rooij et al 2011). This propensity for risk management is particularly significant in the context of retirement planning, where consumers must navigate complex investment decisions to ensure long-term financial security.

Furthermore, financial education can protect consumers from falling victim to fraudulent schemes and predatory financial practices (Braunstein & Welch 2002). Financially educated consumers are better positioned to safeguard their assets and avoid potential financial pitfalls.

Promoting financial inclusion: Financial education plays a vital role in promoting financial inclusion as it empowers individuals from diverse backgrounds to participate more fully in the economy. Research has consistently shown a positive correlation between financial education and increased financial inclusion (Grohmann & Menkhoff 2021). For underserved populations, such as low-income individuals and minorities, financial education can be a stepping stone towards breaking the cycle of poverty and achieving economic mobility (Huston 2010).

Studies have also highlighted the impact of financial education on reducing the gender gap in financial decision making (N26 2024). Educated women tend to be more involved in managing household finances and are better prepared to navigate financial challenges effectively. As financial inclusion grows, the economy benefits from the increased participation and economic contributions of a more diverse consumer base.

Improving retirement preparedness: The ageing population and the shift away from defined benefit pension plans heighten the importance of financial education for retirement preparedness. Individuals are increasingly responsible for managing their retirement savings, making financial literacy a critical determinant of their financial security during retirement (Lusardi & Mitchell 2007).

Research by Bernheim et al (2001) reveals that individuals who receive financial education tend to exhibit higher retirement savings rates and are more likely to make informed decisions about their retirement accounts. Financial education can help consumers understand the importance of starting to save early, the benefits of employer-sponsored retirement plans and the implications of various investment options for their retirement nest egg.

Strengthening the economy: Beyond its impact on individual financial behaviour, financial education also plays a role in bolstering the broader economy. A financially educated population is more likely to participate in the formal financial system, which can lead to increased savings, investment and capital formation (Lusardi & Tufano 2015). As individuals make sound financial choices, they contribute to the stability and efficiency of financial markets.

Furthermore, a financially savvy consumer base can

mitigate the negative effects of financial crises. Research demonstrates that financial education acts as a buffer during economic downturns, as educated individuals are better able to weather financial shocks and maintain their economic wellbeing (eg Bucher-Koenen & Ziegelmeyer 2014). In turn, this economic resilience contributes to a more stable and sustainable economy.

Summary

Financial education holds immense promise as a transformative tool for consumers and society at large. The research overwhelmingly supports the positive impact of financial education on enhancing financial literacy, mitigating financial risks, promoting financial inclusion, improving retirement preparedness and strengthening the economy. Despite this, there are extremely low levels of financial literacy among the common people.

The power of learning by doing

Despite the benefits of financial education being well researched and compelling, there is yet to be an effective model of delivery at scale. The co-owned model has the potential to change this. Issuing shares to customers with easy-to-understand shareholder information has the potential to deliver financial education that's engaging, authentic and real. Rewarding customers with shares for free, for their loyalty, engagement and positive activism (such as digitally voting at AGMs) creates the incentive for customers to engage in financial education. This is also supported by research, as set out below, on the benefits of learning by doing.

The power of practical experience in financial education:
While traditional methods of financial education, such as classroom sessions, have their merits, practical experience offers unique and powerful advantages. Traditional financial education often relies on traditional teaching methods such as lectures and presentations to convey financial concepts and principles. While these methods provide a foundation of knowledge, they often fall short in promoting deeper understanding and application of financial skills (Danes & Hira 1987). Learners may struggle to connect theoretical concepts to real-life scenarios, hindering their ability to apply the knowledge effectively.

Moreover, traditional financial education may not adequately address the psychological and emotional aspects of financial decision making. Behavioural finance research has shown that individuals' financial choices are often influenced by biases, emotions and cognitive limitations (Thaler & Sunstein 2008). Addressing these behavioural factors requires a more immersive and experiential learning approach.

Active learning and retention: Practical experience in financial education leverages the power of active learning, which has been shown to enhance knowledge retention and application. Active learning involves engaging learners in hands-on activities, simulations and real-life scenarios, enabling them to actively participate in the learning process (Cherney 2011).

Research by John Hattie (visible-learning.org) demonstrates that active learning methods lead to higher levels of knowledge retention compared to passive learning approaches. When individuals actively apply financial concepts in real-world situations, they're more likely to remember and internalise the information, making it accessible and applicable in their financial decision making.

Real-life application and decision making: One of the primary benefits of practical experience in financial education is its ability to bridge the gap between theory and real-life application. Learners gain exposure to actual financial scenarios, enabling them to practise decision making in a safe and controlled environment.

Studies have found that individuals who participated in financial education programmes with practical components were more likely to apply the learned concepts in their financial lives (eg De Bruijn et al 2022). By experiencing the consequences of their decisions and witnessing the impact of financial choices, learners can better understand the trade-offs involved, leading to more thoughtful and informed decision making.

Building financial confidence: Financial confidence is a key determinant of individuals' willingness to engage in financial activities and take control of their financial futures (Hilgert et al 2003). Practical experience in financial education fosters a sense of empowerment and self-efficacy, enhancing learners' confidence in managing their finances. When learners successfully navigate financial challenges in a controlled setting, they gain the confidence to tackle real-world financial situations with greater assurance and poise.

Critical thinking: Practical experience in financial education nurtures critical thinking and problem-solving skills, which are essential for making complex financial decisions. Learners are encouraged to analyse financial data, evaluate options and develop strategies to address financial challenges.

A study by Ambuehl et al (2015) reveals that practical financial education programmes foster higher-order thinking skills, enabling individuals to approach financial problems with greater analytical rigour. These cognitive skills extend beyond financial matters and can positively impact other aspects of individuals' lives, enhancing their overall decision-making capabilities.

Behavioural aspects of finance: Financial decisions are influenced not only by objective financial principles but also by behavioural and emotional factors. Practical experience in financial education allows learners to explore their own financial biases and behaviours, making them more self-aware of their financial decision-making processes. Behavioural finance research has shown that individuals often make irrational financial choices due to cognitive biases and emotional responses (Kahneman and Tversky 1979). By experiencing how these biases can influence their financial decisions in a controlled environment, learners can develop strategies to mitigate their impact in real-life situations.

Encouraging lifelong learning: Practical experience in financial education fosters a culture of lifelong learning, encouraging individuals to continuously seek knowledge and improve their financial skills. Learners become more receptive to financial information and are motivated to seek out additional resources and educational opportunities.

As financial markets and economic conditions evolve, this inclination towards continuous learning becomes increasingly important in helping individuals adapt and make informed financial decisions in changing environments.

Although it's abundantly clear from all this research that financial education is a good thing, many models still fail to deliver meaningful benefits. Co-owned offers an immediate way to change that: real-life experience for consumers of having investments that the poverty trap might otherwise have prevented them from ever gaining. Another clear advantage is that this experience is delivered in a natural way, as a by-product of their normal consumer behaviour, and therefore not perceived as a paternalistic or 'forced' educational situation.

Changing behaviours

Even with higher levels of financial education and financial literacy, changing behaviours is hard. As I have mentioned, popular culture has encouraged a 'spend first and save and invest later' attitude, with later rarely coming. It's hard to change cultural habits and it's getting harder over generations, with most parents unable to teach their children good financial habits, especially when it comes to saving and investing, especially if it's not something they do themselves.

At Salary Finance, we identified an important behavioural dynamic. When we gave employees the option to set up a payroll-deducted savings account, only 1–2 per cent would sign up. This is the group of employees who were typically already good at managing their money. They saw the product as an opportunity to save first and spend later. If the money didn't hit their current account (as we deducted savings straight from payroll and put it into a savings account for them), they would be less likely to spend it. We tried many times to encourage more employees to use this savings product but with little success. The common reason given was that employees didn't have the money to save.

After a few years, we had a breakthrough. We identified that, when employees were taking a payroll-deducted loan, if we asked whether they'd like us to keep that same payroll deduction going after the loan was paid off and use it to move funds to a savings account, 40 per cent agreed. Interestingly, when we asked an employee if they had money for savings, they said no. But if we asked if they could afford loan repayments, they said yes. When we asked if we could continue loan repayments into saving payments, many said yes, as it resonated more with them in the context of loan repayments, something they were more familiar with.

My hope is that a similar dynamic will occur with Co-owned. The common person is familiar with spending money and reward schemes. By putting them together in the form of share rewards, I believe it could unconsciously help people to learn about investing and be the start of their investment journey, which they can then build on. With Salary Finance, most of our savers never thought they had the money to save. After setting up their payroll-deducted savings account and typically forgetting about it for a few months, they had a few hundred pounds in savings by that point – and then their mindset about savings completely changed. They were then focused on getting to a thousand pounds or more in savings and we had managed to change their psychology around saving being a possibility. My hope is that, through co-owned, we can also change the psychology of how the common person thinks about investing.

Conclusion

The automatic issuance of share rewards to consumers creates the opportunity to engage consumers in financial education, which in turn creates a multitude of benefits. Importantly, this includes promoting a long-term investment mindset. Traditional consumer behaviour often focuses on short-term gratification and immediate consumption. However, when consumers become shareholders, they will naturally develop a vested interest in the company's performance over time.

The benefits of practical financial education extend beyond individual consumers, positively impacting society. A financially literate and empowered population contributes to a more stable and resilient economy, reduces the burden on public assistance programmes and fosters a culture of responsible financial decision making. As consumers learn about how big businesses work (as a co-shareholder), it can also help to spark their own entrepreneurial ideas and confidence in launching their own businesses.

Co-owned has the potential to transform the financial lives of the common person directly (financially) as well as indirectly (knowledge and education). This creates direct benefits for society at large (economic growth, detailed in the next chapter), as well as indirect benefits, with financially healthy individuals statistically being mentally and physically healthier also, with associated benefits. Let's look at how this can be achieved.

10

The benefits for government and society

Business cannot succeed in societies that fail.
— Paul Poleman, former CEO of Unilever

As Archie Norman, a prominent British businessman and former politician, recently put it in the *Financial Times* (Norman 2023), 'The bond between British business and society has eroded.' I believe he's right. This chapter explores why as well as how co-owned can bring them closer together. It also looks at the impact on government when business and society are divided and how Co-owned can help the government achieve its goals.

The divide between business and society

Today, despite the enormous influence business has on society, it seems as if society doesn't have a stake in business. This isn't just a feeling. As we saw in Chapter 3, in the UK in the 1960s, residents owned more than 50 per cent of the country's listed company shares. Today, that number stands at 12 per cent. Pension schemes are shifting too, holding fewer equities and even fewer UK ones. Even those that do invest in the stock market demonstrate a disconnect, with more than 40 per cent of all shareholdings being held through nominee platforms (holding the shares on behalf of the customer). For the underlying retail shareholders, nominee platforms result in a lack of communication, personal connection and, most of the time, voting on company resolutions. An analogy is attending a party where everyone is wearing a mask. You don't know who they are or what they want and you can't talk to them. It doesn't lead to connection.

Archie Norman, current chair of British retailer Marks

& Spencer (M&S), describes the close-knit community that M&S used to enjoy with direct retail shareholders. 'We knew them and they knew us.' But times have changed. M&S can no longer reach 70 per cent of its private shareholders directly. And every year, they watch 4,000 'known' shareholders slip through their fingers due to the nominee accounts being intermediaries (Norman 2023).

Even if companies could reach their retail shareholders, their investor relations teams aren't set up to communicate with them in an engaging way. Annual reports now run to hundreds of pages; they're designed for sophisticated institutional investors and are largely indecipherable to the common person. This all leads to companies being seen as impersonal and complex, hence the lack of connection between society and business.

Rebuilding the bond requires a paradigm shift in how companies view and advance investor relations – from focusing solely on a relatively small number of sophisticated institutional investors to putting in just as much effort with the general public. By focusing on their customers, they build on a connection they already have. While one customer shareholder isn't as valuable as an institutional shareholder, when individuals act collectively, they can make a big difference and, ultimately, move share prices. For most companies with a retail customer base, it generally won't take much investment per customer for customers to collectively become one of the biggest shareholders in the company.

To build back the connection between business and society, society needs to have more stake in business. That means more direct communication channels and content geared for retail investors. All of this requires a new focus for investor relations teams.

The growing influence of business

Since the early 2000s, there has been an acceleration in the power of business, driven by its increasingly monopolistic nature. Figure 28 shows the combined market share of the two largest companies in various industries in the US in the early 2000s vs today.

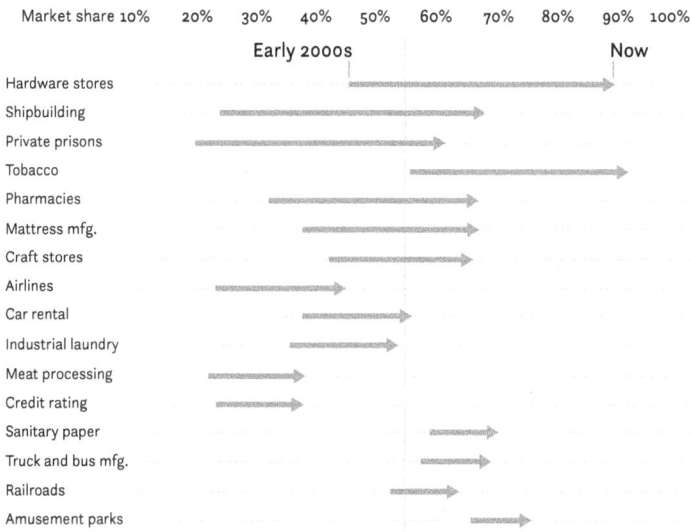

Figure 28: Combined market share of the two largest companies by industry in the US in the early 2000s vs today

Across the range of sectors shown, there has been significant consolidation of market share in the top two players. This gives these companies more political power because they control more jobs and more resources, as well as having more commercial power to set prices and wages. And unsurprisingly, the beneficiaries are their shareholders. Figure 29 shows the total return of US companies that have an economic moat (Warren Buffett's term for a competitive advantage in the form of a monopolistic market) versus the market as a whole, with the former consistently delivering higher returns.

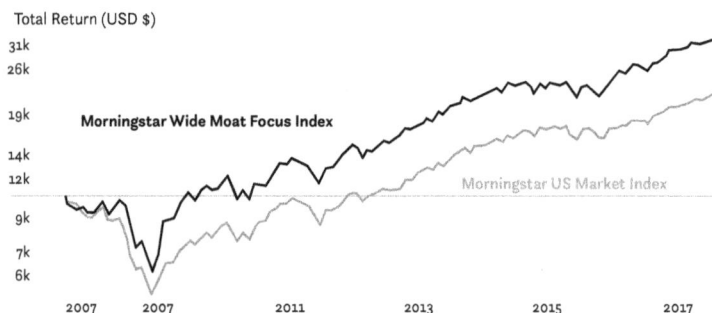

Total Return (USD $)

Morningstar Wide Moat Focus Index

Morningstar US Market Index

| 31k | 26k | 19k | 14k | 12k | 9k | 7k | 6k |

2007   2007   2011   2013   2015   2017

Figure 29: Total return of companies with a moat vs those that don't

The power of business in society today is most starkly shown in technology. The value of the five biggest tech companies now accounts for almost a quarter of the value of the entire US stock market. In addition to the stock market, these tech companies have a much wider control over society. In the US, Amazon is the first stop for almost a third of all US consumers, Apple has 43 per cent of the smartphone market in the US, and Google and Facebook are the first stop for many (if not most) Americans in search of news. In a world where business, and in particular big business, controls so much of society, bringing them closer together for the common good has never been more important.

Adding democratic decision making

As companies grow in size and influence, their governance becomes a matter of national (and international) interest. While the role of regulators is to ensure consumer protection, they're generally ill equipped to do this. Talented regulators are increasingly lured by higher-paid jobs at the companies they were once regulating. The scale and complexity of big business relative to the resources of regulators rarely match, leaving a string of major regulators failing to spot systemically important issues across sectors. And the fines that regulators can impose are often limited and accounted for as a manageable cost of business.

In 2022, two US academics wrote an academic paper titled 'How retail investing improves corporate governance and benefits society' (Ricci & Sautter 2022). Their conclusions apply equally to customer shareholders and are summarised below.

The pandemic created a rise in retail investors in the US. They are typically younger and more diverse than traditional investors, with a 2020 study showing that 58 per cent are white, 17 per cent African American, 15 per cent Hispanic/Latino, and 10 per cent Asian, with women making up 37 per cent of new retail investors. A quarter of retail investors earn less than $35,000 a year (the average salary in the US is $59,000).

The paper sets out the case for these retail investors, who more closely represent society than the typical shareholders I have been discussing, to have a vote and a real say in how the companies they're invested in are run. The digital world we now live in makes this possible but it requires a corporate governance infrastructure designed to enable it, as well as companies that want to embrace it. Retail investors, especially customer investors, have the potential to make corporations more approachable, more accountable and more in tune with what matters to society. While this is good for society, I also believe it's good for business. While companies may see regulators as interfering and employees as replaceable, the reality is that companies are reliant on their customers. And if they're going to take tough feedback from anyone, I don't think there's anyone better than their customers to give it.

The power of retail investors acting as a collective

Companies haven't traditionally focused on retail investors, as individual retail investors don't move the needle (ie the share price). However, when individual retail investors form a collective, they certainly do move the needle. There's an opportunity for companies to harness collective power, benefiting customers and society.

The story of GameStop brings to life the impact coordinated individuals can have on a public company. In January 2021, the US video game, consumer electronics and gaming merchandise retailer GameStop's share price soared by 2,000 per cent as amateur traders zeroed in on the stock, betting against hedge funds that had been shorting it (ie betting that a company's share price will fall). This rally was driven by collective action among retail investors who coordinated on platforms such as Reddit's r/wallstreetbets forum (Davies 2021).

The GameStop case highlights the impact retail investors can have when they perform as a collective. The combination of technological innovation, social media coordination and the demographics of new investors has created a dynamic that seasoned market professionals are still trying to understand. GameStop's story isn't an outlier but a symbol of a transformative shift in market dynamics that has far-reaching implications for investing, regulation and market behaviour. Co-owned companies that create the infrastructure to engage with their customer shareholders can unleash the potential benefit for the companies themselves as well as the wider society.

Why governments should care

Governments exist to organise and maintain order within a society, providing a framework for social cooperation. Their primary functions include making and enforcing laws to ensure individual rights, public safety and social welfare. Governments also oversee the provision of public goods and services such as education, healthcare and transport and manage economic policies to regulate commerce, protect consumers and promote overall economic stability. By balancing the interests of various groups and individuals, governments aim to create a fair and just society where citizens can live, work and prosper.

When the economic system (in this case capitalism) isn't working because business (shareholders) and society (the common people) are at odds, it makes it difficult to govern. While shareholders are much fewer in number, they wield power through where and how they choose to deploy their resources. And while the common person lacks power, they make up for this in their number and their voices. This tension between two parts of society means governments often end up fighting fires, attempting to appease and reconcile these two groups.

The answer lies in bringing business and society onto the same side and ensuring capitalism is a system that uplifts everyone for the common good, enabling governments to move beyond firefighting. Co-owned has the potential to achieve this. Rather than choosing policies that solely benefit shareholders or the common person, governments can focus on initiatives that drive economic growth at a national level, knowing that it will benefit society as a whole. Interventions made today – for example, assessing whether banks and energy companies are making too much profit in a cost of living crisis – can instead be voted on by customer co-shareholders. Customers, better than anyone, can represent public opinion. Likewise, co-owned can drive productivity and as a result economic growth: both are issues the UK has long been struggling with.

Economic growth is achieved through an increase in the production and consumption of goods and services within an economy over time. It's typically measured by the rise in the gross domestic product (GDP), which sums up the total value of all goods and services produced within a country during a specific period. Economic growth reflects the ability of an economy to increase its capacity to produce, providing more goods and services to consumers, more job opportunities and generally a higher standard of living. Growth is often seen as a key indicator of the economic health and vitality of a nation.

Productivity refers to the efficiency with which inputs (such as labour, capital and technology) are transformed into outputs (such as goods and services). In the context of economic growth, an increase in productivity means that more output can be produced with the same amount of input. Higher productivity often leads to increased profitability for businesses, higher wages for workers and overall economic expansion, as resources are utilised more effectively.

Co-owned has the potential to improve productivity by fast-tracking customer-led innovation cycles. If customers are incentivised to help grow the companies they already use, they're more likely to provide high-quality input. That means they can help companies to build more products that consumers want, which can be sold both domestically and internationally. In parallel, this reduces waste from failed products by incentivising early customer feedback. The collective power of customer input to drive innovation creates a new paradigm that drives productivity and growth.

If the UK and US governments backed co-owned, it would also provide a much-needed impetus for more companies to list on their stock exchange, providing an additional source of liquidity for companies to grow. As mentioned earlier in this book, a nation with more broadly spread wealth and financial health also has positive impacts on both physical and mental health. There are a number of studies supporting this, with some included below.

Financial stress and health outcomes: Research by Sweet et al (2013) in *Social Science and Medicine* set out that financial stress often leads to poor health outcomes. This connection manifests through chronic stress, anxiety and depression, which can, in turn, lead to physical health problems such as heart disease and hypertension.

Impact of financial interventions on health: A study by Haushofer and Shapiro (2016) found that providing unconditional cash transfers to households in Kenya significantly reduced stress levels and improved wellbeing. The researchers used levels of cortisol (a stress hormone) to measure changes, indicating a tangible physiological connection between financial health and physical wellbeing.

The socioeconomic gradient in health: The Whitehall Studies by Marmot et al (1991) have shown a clear gradient in health according to socioeconomic status within the UK. The higher the economic status, the better the health outcomes, demonstrating a link between financial prosperity and physical health.

Health investments and financial stability: Various studies have underscored that financially stable individuals are more likely to invest in their health (eg Lolokote et al 2017). This includes more regular check-ups, adherence to medication and healthy lifestyle choices, leading to improved overall physical health.

All of these reasons, individually and combined, create a compelling case for governments to support co-owned.

Increasing retail participation in equity markets

At the time of writing, there was increasing comment from UK politicians (from both major political parties) on the importance of widening retail participation in equity markets. Put simply, it's important for more of the general population to own shares in companies – in the UK, particularly British companies (hosted on the London Stock Exchange) – either directly or indirectly (through funds). While it's true that such participation is currently a problem, there remains a real lack of innovation regarding potential solutions that can move the dial. I believe co-owned is an important part of the answer and I'm excited about sharing my thinking with the UK and US governments through the publication of this book. Here I set out some of the latest research on retail (ie common person) participation in the equity markets and why it's important. It draws on insightful research from the New Financial think tank (Bierbaum & Singhal 2023). Retail participation in equity markets can mean different things to different people, such as encouraging more people to:

→ buy shares in a company
→ buy shares in an active or passive fund

- trade shares
- contribute more to their pensions and making more active choices regarding their pensions
- vote in AGMs and make use of their stewardship rights.

While all these dimensions are important for a prosperous society, I've focused on retail participation in equity markets encouraging more people to buy (own) shares directly in companies, vote in AGMs and use their stewardship rights. If we can encourage the general population to meaningfully participate in this way, the other areas (which are just as important) will naturally follow.

The share of UK households directly owning shares has halved from 2003 to 2022, from 23 per cent to 11 per cent. While Britain is the biggest financial market in Europe, the same dynamic is true in most European countries, with Germany, Italy and Poland all having less than 10 per cent of households directly owning stocks and shares in 2022. The one exception is Sweden, where 22 per cent of households directly owned stocks in 2022. This is attributed to high adoption of tech to make investing easier and more engaging, a simple and low flat annual tax on investments, and a healthy ecosystem and supply of capital for small and medium-sized businesses (SMEs) planning to list on the local stock exchange. These are all interventions that the UK and other European governments should consider (and make/support), but even with these, 22 per cent leaves significant room for growth. If UK households were more like Swedish households and invested a significant proportion of their assets in equities and funds, this would unlock an additional £740 billion of capital that could support the British economy.

The government is right to be focusing on the lack of common person participation in retail equity markets. It represents a huge societal opportunity: for the common person to increase their long-term financial wellbeing; for companies issuing shares to connect with society in a new way; and for the capital markets and financial services industries to connect with millions of households and help them make the most of their money.

In the UK, for many individuals, investment equals risk and risk equals losing money. The loss aversion is understandable, particularly in the current cost of living crisis, but unfortunately people often place too little emphasis on the returns side of the equation and too much emphasis on the likelihood of losing money from investing. This is especially the case over longer-term horizons, where the general public also underestimates (or is unaware of) how the value of their money is eroding due to inflation when sitting in savings accounts with low interest (or worse, where consumers choose to spend discretionally over saving or investing). For reference, according to analysis by IG (Bright 2022), the annualised return of the FTSE 100 (including reinvested dividends) from its inception in 1984 to 2022 was 7.5 per cent and in the ten years to 2022 it was 6.3 per cent. Investing can be a powerful tool for individuals to improve their long-term financial wellbeing and to take a share of the wider economic growth that they help create. The US has a more open and positive attitude to investing in shares but there remains almost the same level of opportunity, with only 21 per cent of households owning shares directly.

Governments can help

There is an action the UK and US governments can take to jump-start the adoption of co-owned. That action is to offer tax breaks to companies that issue shares to their customers as rewards, so it becomes cost neutral for them. If there's one thing that all companies love, it's paying less tax, and this would almost guarantee widespread adoption overnight. There could be some simple rules added, such as the requirements of customers to take part in corporate governance, which would further the government agenda in other necessary areas too. For co-owned customers, making capital gains tax-free would also accelerate adoption and support the government agenda of diverting more retail money into public companies to help them grow. In the UK, this could be done relatively easily by extending the ISA scheme.

11

Implementing Co-owned and the role of AI

Vision without action is merely a dream.
Action without vision just passes the time.
Vision with action can change the world.
— Joel Arthur Barker, American futurist

Having made it this far into the book, I hope you're as excited as I am about the potential for the co-owned model to realign capitalism for the common good. Of course, as the creator of Co-owned, I'm passionate about its potential. But what gives me the most confidence is not my passion (everyone likes their own ideas) but the overwhelmingly positive feedback I've received from the smartest and most brutally honest people I know, from Harvard and Columbia Business School academics to prominent British and American politicians, to FTSE 100 and Fortune 500 CEOs and executives, to personal finance experts who understand the realities of life for the common person.

The official launch of this book, which took place at the World Economic Forum (WEF) in Davos, also marks the launch of a new organisation I have founded called Co-owned, a research and technology organisation whose mission is to create a 'revolution in retail investment by enabling companies to turn their customers into co-share-holders'. Put simply, Co-owned, the organisation, will help companies on their path to becoming co-owned, through enabling research and technology.

As we build Co-owned, I'm excited to put into practice the learnings from the two successful social purpose start-ups that I've founded previously, and this time share more of the journey along the way, not just at the end. This chapter sets out how we can make Co-owned happen and make it a success for the common good.

Research division

One of the most important lessons I've learned about scaling organisations is the importance of data to guide decision making. The research division within Co-owned will focus on gathering and analysing data to help guide companies on how to best implement the co-owned model, to evidence its impact and continually optimise.

In the first instance, we'll partner with companies to conduct statistically significant studies like the Columbia Business School study featured in Chapter 5, to assess the impact customer co-ownership can have on key business metrics such as customer loyalty (retention), customer spend (share of wallet) and customer engagement.

We plan to do this by picking a sample of customers in each partner company and running a pilot programme. This can be an official pilot where the company is issuing the shares and paying for the rewards, or it can be an unofficial pilot run by Co-owned, where we identify a cohort of customers and pay for the issuance of shares to demonstrate the benefits and build the business case for the company.

During the pilot phase, as well as proving the overall benefit and impact on key business metrics, we will also 'test and learn' different implementation models (examples below) to determine the optimal one.

Implementation models

There are many ways in which a company can implement the co-owned model. Companies that will enjoy the most success are the ones that employ effective implementation and adopt an innovative approach led by data and research.

Example implementation models include:

➡ giving all customers shares for free with no strings attached

- rewarding customers with shares as they make purchases
- giving customers discounted shares for new share purchases
- rewarding certain behaviours (such as upgrading to a premium account) with shares.

There are also important decisions to be made such as whether to offer shares immediately or require a hold or vesting period. Each model has its advantages and disadvantages and a pilot 'test and learn' programme can help companies determine which will best meet their business objectives.

A core emphasis of the research division will be behavioural science, to ensure the design of the programme meets the intended outcomes. If the programme is designed poorly, customers could become overly sensitive to share price movements. But if it's designed well, customers will feel a loyalty to the company that transcends day-to-day transactional share price movements.

Technology division

The technology division within Co-owned will create technology that minimises friction and maximises the impact of any Co-owned implementation model. Rather than each company building their own technology, Co-owned will deliver a modern, world-class platform for companies and their customers, leaving companies to focus on the data to decide how best to implement and optimise the model. A core part of the technology solution will come together in a new app called Stock Rewards. Stock Rewards includes the following functionality.

Signing up customers: Companies can issue their customers with marketing material and, for example, include a simple QR code from which they can download the Stock Rewards app. The app will enable the customer to create a share account.

Acquiring shares: The app will allow customers to acquire shares in companies they choose, using their own cash or redeeming rewards offered by companies. Those rewards will automatically be visible on the app.

Round-ups: App users will be able to link their bank account(s) and the app will automatically flag when a user is spending money in a public company in which they can acquire shares and/or a company offering share rewards. App users can choose to automatically round up their spending in public companies to acquire further shares in that company, setting spending and risk limits of their choosing.

Coaching: App users will receive content on how shares work and how to analyse a company's performance as well as risk level to help set investment parameters in line with their risk tolerance. Co-owned will also use this as a way to increase general financial literacy.

Engagement: Companies will have the opportunity to engage with their customer shareholders through the app. This could be to seek feedback on products, to provide customer input on corporate governance decisions or to take part in digital AGMs.

Shareholder votes: Customer shareholders will be notified when there are shareholder motions to vote on, explaining what they are and allowing them to vote simply through the app.

Digital AGM: Annual general meetings will be livestreamed through the app to allow customer shareholders to view them (in real time or later) and the opportunity to ask questions or take part in real-time votes.

The role of AI in bringing business closer to customers

As mentioned in the last chapter, there's an increasing recognition that investor relations documentation is currently geared for sophisticated institutional investors and not retail investors. The answer isn't to stop producing the information required by sophisticated institutional investors but to also produce content that's engaging and useful for retail customers. This requires the investor relations team to develop a new skill. While the information required by institutional investors is largely homogenous, the same isn't true for retail investors. Retail investors (customers in this instance) can be as diverse as society, with different levels of starting knowledge, different preferences in how they receive information and different depths of interest. Generative AI has the potential to take company information and deliver it to a retail audience in a personalised way. It can tailor the communications based on the level of knowledge of the customer, provide the level of detail they're interested in and deliver it in an engaging form For example, AI could be used to produce a personalised monthly podcast for each Stock Reward app user, summarising how the companies they are co-owners of are performing, and also featuring companies they're spending their money on but are yet to own shares in.

Users could choose how long they'd like this to be and set out their level of knowledge so that the content is tailored accordingly. AI is, of course, an area that's rapidly evolving and appropriate safeguards will be required.

Customer co-owners fund

As we saw in Chapter 6, when you look at the major share-holders of public companies, you typically see a list of institutional investment funds. We'll know when we're succeeding when, towards the top of the shareholder list, is a new fund called 'Customer Co-owners Fund'. Rather than retailers issuing shares directly to customers, they'll be given a share in the 'Customer Co-owners Fund' with a value matching their underlying share value. They'll be the ultimate beneficial owners of the shares but, to enable collective customer action with ease of administration, all customer shares will be held through this fund. Companies will be able to communicate with all their underlying shareholders, in line with the communications consents provided by the customers. All of this will be managed through the Stock Rewards app. This structure will enable customers to act as a collective with a pooled shareholding.

Winning clients

My previous company, Salary Finance, went from an idea to a business that today partners with 20 per cent of the FTSE 100, nine of the ten largest retailers, two in three hospitals and many more, and in the US, partners with 500,000 employers. The playbook we used to achieve this will be repeated for Co-owned. Salary Finance focuses on helping companies help their employees to become financially healthier and happier because it's good for employees, companies and society.

Becoming co-owned is a board and CEO-level matter. Alongside launching this book, we'll be writing to the boards, CEOs and heads of investor relations at every listed company in the UK and then the US with a copy of this book. In addition to listed companies, we'll also be targeting private equity firms and private equity-backed companies. Then, in each sector, we'll select a launch partner. While the launch partner takes a leap of faith in going first, they also benefit from first-mover advantage.

The Co-owned business model will include charging businesses for the research projects (to determine the value to them of being co-owned) and the consumer technology which will enable them to become co-owned.

Once we've proven ourselves in each sector, we'll then roll out to other companies in the sector. Our work will focus on partnering with forward-thinking companies that see the value for business and society in being co-owned. Sectors with particular relevance for Co-owned are those where there's a high number of individual customers. This includes retail, supermarkets, utilities (water, tele-communications, energy), transport, travel, banking and insurance. We always think big and one of our first targets is X, which involves setting out the case to Elon Musk as to why X should be user 'co-owned'.

12

Conclusion

*You can't go back and make a new start, but you can
start right now and make a brand new ending.*
— James R Sherman, *Rejection*

Imagine a world where...

... a company that you're a customer of makes a profit and you feel happy because you also share in some of the rewards.

... the government reports that the economy is growing and you feel happy knowing that some of that will benefit you and your wealth.

... you have a seat at the table of the companies you spend your money on and they ask for your input on key decisions.

... you help the companies you use with new ideas and, when those succeed, you benefit as a co-owner of the company.

... rather than just being a customer, you're an owner and are made to feel like one with special rewards.

... there's less division between business and society – we're all on the same side and the government doesn't need to continuously firefight.

... you learn about how companies and investing work in an engaging and safe way, helping you to build wealth for your family with minimal effort.

... the norm, not the exception, is that your children will be wealthier than you.

... society moves from idolising those people and companies with vast amounts of money to those people and companies who make others wealthy.

Sound good? Welcome to the world of co-owned.

Alternatively, imagine the world if the status quo continues...

... the wealth gap between shareholders (the 1 per cent) and the common person (the 99 per cent) continues to grow.

... workers continue to see a decline in wealth despite working more and more and each generation becoming less and less well off.

... instead of one in three children living in poverty, that turns to two in three.

... where society is no longer willing to accept mass impoverishment and mass social unrest ensues to the detriment of all, with authoritarian leaders on the rise.

... where the government increases tax for business, causing more companies to relocate, and reducing innovation and growth.

There really isn't much of a contest, is there?

Help to make Co-owned happen.

If you're a shareholder or executive at a public or investor-backed company, talk to us and we'll help you become co-owned.

If you're a worker, write to the chair of your board and executives in your company and introduce the co-owned idea and this book to them.

If you work in government, speak to your treasury colleagues and ask them to back the movement, with tax cuts for companies that become co-owned.

Join the Co-owned community by signing up at Co-owned.com to keep updated on our latest developments.

See you there!

References

Accenture (2016) 'Members of customer loyalty programs generate significantly more revenue for retailers than do non-members, Accenture research finds'. URL: newsroom.accenture.com/news/2016/ members-of-customer-loyalty-programs-generate-significantly-more-revenue-for-retailers-than-do-non-members-accenture-research-finds

Allison, T (2018) 'Financial health of young America: update'. Young Invincibles. URL: younginvincibles.org/wp-content/uploads/2018/04/ Financial-Health-of-Young-America-update.pdf

Ambuehl, S, Bernheim, B D & Lusardi, A (2015) 'The effect of financial education on the quality of decision making'. Global Finance Literacy Excellence Center. URL: gflec.org/wp-content/uploads/2016/08/ WP-2015-4-The-Effect-of-Financial-Education-on-the-Quality-of-Decision-Making.pdf

Antavo (2022) 'The North America customer loyalty report'. URL: antavo. com/reports/north-america-customer-loyalty-report-2022

Bernheim, B D, Skinner, J & Weinberg, S (2001) 'What accounts for the variation in retirement wealth among US households?' *The American Economic Review* 91(4).

Bialik, K & Fry, R (2019) 'Millennial life: how young adulthood today compares with prior generations'. Pew Research Center. URL: pewresearch.org/social-trends/2019/02/14/ millennial-life-how-young-adulthood-today-compares-with-prior-generations-2

Bierbaum, M & Singhal, S (2023) 'Report – widening retail participation in equity markets'. New Financial. URL: newfinancial.org/publications-1/ widening-retail-participation-in-equity-markets

Bond Brand Loyalty (2022) 'After years behind masks, consumers just want to be "seen"'. URL: info.bondbrandloyalty.com/theloyaltyreport2022

Braunstein, S & Welch, C (2002) 'Financial literacy: an overview of practice, research and policy'. *Federal Reserve Bulletin* 88.

Bright, A (2022) 'What are the average returns of the FTSE 100?'. IG. URL: ig.com/uk/trading-strategies/what-are-the-average-returns-of-the-ftse-100--230511

BT (2023) 'Results for the full year to 31 March 2023' and Annual

Report 2023. URL: newsroom.bt.com/results-for-the-full-year-to-31-march-2023 *and* bt.com/bt-plc/assets/documents/investors/financial-reporting-and-news/annual-reports/2023/2023-bt-group-plc-annual-report.pdf

Bucher-Koenen, T & Ziegelmeyer, M (2014) 'Once burned, twice shy? Financial literacy and wealth losses during the financial crisis'. *Review of Finance* 18(6).

BusinessWire (2013) 'Nielsen survey: 84 percent of global respondents more likely to visit retailers that offer a loyalty program'. URL: businesswire.com/news/home/20131111006099/en/Nielsen-Survey-84-Percent-of-Global-Respondents-More-Likely-to-Visit-Retailers-That-Offer-a-Loyalty-Program

Cherney, I D (2011) 'Active learning' in *Promoting Student Engagement*, Society for the Teaching of Psychology.

Chisholm, J (2023) 'Global buybacks surged to record $1.3 trillion in 2022, almost eclipsing dividends'. MarketWatch. URL: marketwatch.com/story/global-buybacks-surged-to-record-1-3-trillion-in-2022-almost-eclipsing-dividends-d18be151

Colley, N (2023) 'Millennials are seeing their net worth go down. Student loans play a huge role'. *Forbes*. URL: forbes.com/sites/nataliecolley/2023/03/17/student-loans-impact-on-millennial-net-worth-the-importance-of-strategic-college-financing/?sh=2f402e693516

Columbia Business School (2021) 'Owning a company's stock drives brand loyalty and increases spending'. URL: business.columbia.edu/press-releases/cbs-press-releases/owning-companys-stock-drives-brand-loyalty-and-increases-spending

Danes, S M & Hira, T K (1987) 'Money management knowledge of college students'. *Journal of Student Financial Aid* 17.

Davies, R (2021) 'GameStop: how Reddit amateurs took aim at Wall Street's short-sellers'. *The Guardian* 28/1/21. URL: theguardian.com/business/2021/jan/28/gamestop-how-reddits-amateurs-tripped-wall-streets-short-sellers

De Bruijn, E-J, Antonides, G & Madern, T (2022) 'A behaviourally informed financial education program for the financially vulnerable: design and effectiveness'. *Frontiers in Psychology* 13.

Deloitte (2018) '2018 Deloitte millennial survey'. URL: deloitte.com/content/dam/Deloitte/global/Documents/About-Deloitte/gx-2018-millennial-survey-report.pdf

Dudley, T & Rouen, E (2021a) 'Employee ownership and wealth inequality: a path to reducing wealth concentration'. Harvard Business School. URL: hbs.edu/faculty/Pages/item.aspx?num=61313

Dudley, T & Rouen, E (2021b) 'The big benefits of employee ownership'. Harvard Business Review. URL: hbr.org/2021/05/the-big-benefits-of-employee-ownership

Economic Policy Institute (2022) 'The productivity–pay gap'. URL: epi.org/productivity-pay-gap

Faria, J (2023) 'Loyalty programs and marketing in the US: statistics & facts'. Statista. URL: statista.com/topics/7986/loyalty-programs-in-the-us

Federal Reserve System (2022) 'Economic well-being of US households in 2022'. URL: federalreserve.gov/publications/files/2022-report-economic-well-being-us-households-202305.pdf

Feger, A (2023) 'Sephora's loyalty SVP shares tips on creating a best-in-class loyalty program'. Emarketer. URL: emarketer.com/content/sephora-s-loyalty-svp-shares-tips-on-creating-best-in-class-loyalty-program

Francis-Devine, B (2024) 'Poverty in the UK: statistics'. House of Commons Library. URL: researchbriefings.files.parliament.uk/documents/SN07096/SN07096.pdf

Gallo, A (2014) 'The value of keeping the right customers'. *Harvard Business Review*. URL: hbr.org/2014/10/the-value-of-keeping-the-right-customers

Gill, A & Daw, E (2017) 'From care to where? Care leavers' access to accommodation'. Centrepoint. URL: centrepoint.org.uk/research-reports/care-where-care-leavers-access-accommodation

Green, D (2018) 'Prime members spend way more on Amazon than other customers – and the difference is growing'. Business Insider. URL: businessinsider.com/amazon-prime-customers-spend-more-than-others-2018-10

Grohmann, A & Menkhoff, L (2021) 'The relationship between financial literacy and financial inclusion' in *The Routledge Handbook of Financial Literacy*, Routledge.

Hastings, J S, Madrian, B C & Skimmyhorn, W L (2013) 'Financial literacy, financial education and economic outcomes'. *Annual Review of Economics* 5(1).

Haushofer, J & Shapiro, J (2016) 'The short-term impact of unconditional cash transfers to the poor: experimental evidence from Kenya'. *The Quarterly Journal of Economics* 131(4).

Hearne, E, Crouch, E et al (2023) 'Loyalty programs need next-generation design'. Boston Consulting Group. URL: bcg.com/publications/2023/loyalty-programs-need-to-continue-to-evolve

Hilgert, M A, Hogarth, J M & Beverly, S (2003) 'Household financial management: the connection between knowledge and behaviour'. *Federal Reserve Bulletin* 89.

Huston, S J (2010) 'Measuring financial literacy'. *The Journal of Consumer Affairs* June 2010.

Icahn, C (nd) URL: carlicahn.com

Johnston, L (2022) 'Adidas leans into memberships and beefs up digital hires'. Consumer Goods Technology. URL: consumergoods.com/adidas-leans-memberships-and-beefs-digital-hires

Kahneman, D & Tversky, A (1979) 'Prospect theory: an analysis of decision under risk'. *Econometrica* 47(2).

Kube, S, Maréchal, M A & Puppe, C (2012). 'The currency of reciprocity: gift exchange in the workplace'. *American Economic Review* 102.

Lee, J (2023) '37.9 million Americans are living in poverty, according to the US Census. But the problem could be far worse'. CNBC. URL: cnbc.com/2023/03/07/why-poverty-might-be-far-worse-in-the-us-than-its-reported.html

Li, X & Petrick, J F (2008) 'Examining the antecedents of brand loyalty from an investment model perspective'. *Journal of Travel Research* 47.

Lolokote, S, Hebtemariam Hidru, T & Li, X (2017) 'Do socio-cultural factors influence college students' self-rated health status and health-promoting lifestyles? A cross-sectional multicenter study in Dalian, China'. *BMC Public Health* 17.

Louch, W & Levingston, I (2023) 'Private equity takes a renewed interest in UK plc'. URL: ft.com/content/d60d6866-920d-4617-a693-0f73b3f24eea

Luhby, T. (2020) 'Many millennials are worse off than their parents – a first in American history'. CNN. URL: edition.cnn.com/2020/01/11/politics/millennials-income-stalled-upward-mobility-us

Lusardi, A & Mitchell, O (2007) 'Financial literacy and retirement preparedness: evidence and implications for financial education'. *Business Economics* 42(1).

Lusardi, A & Mitchell, O (2014) 'The economic importance of financial literacy: theory and evidence'. *Journal of Economic Literature* 52(1).

Lusardi, A & Tufano, P (2015) 'Debt literacy, financial experiences and overindebtedness'. *Journal of Pension Economics and Finance* 14(4).

Marmot, M G, Smith, G D et al (1991) 'Health inequalities among British civil servants: the Whitehall II study'. *The Lancet* 337(8754).

Medina, P, Mittal, V & Pagel, M (2021) 'The effect of stock ownership on individual spending and loyalty'. National Bureau of Economic Research. URL: nber.org/system/files/working_papers/w28479/w28479.pdf

Miller, G (2022) 'Customer retention analysis: the indispensable metrics you need to know'. URL: web.archive.org/web/20221130230858/https://www.annexcloud.com/blog/customer-retention-technology-analysis

Mitchell, O S & Lusardi, A (eds) (2011) *Financial literacy: implications for retirement security and the financial marketplace*. Oxford University Press.

MyBnk (nd) 'Our work'. URL: mybnk.org/our-work/financial-education

N26 (2024) 'Women and financial literacy: closing the gender gap'. URL: n26.com/en-eu/blog/women-and-financial-literacy-closing-the-gender-gap

Nathan, D (2024) 'Carnival, Whitbread and Legal & General – looking beyond the shareholder perks'. Hargreaves Lansdown. URL: hl.co.uk/news/carnival-whitbread-and-legal-general-looking-beyond-the-shareholder-perks

Norman, A (2023) 'The bond between British business and society has eroded'. *Financial Times*. URL: ft.com/content/31cdof86-0304-43ab-a39d-a2988c806b14

O'Brien, L (2024) 'UK savings account statistics 2024'. Money.co.uk. URL: money.co.uk/savings-accounts/savings-statistics/uk-savings-account-statistics

O'Brien, L & Jones, C (1995) 'Do rewards really create loyalty?'. Harvard Business Review May–June 1995. URL: hbr.org/1995/05/do-rewards-really-create-loyalty

ONS (2021) 'UK shares and private pension wealth by household income'. URL: ons.gov.uk/peoplepopulationandcommunity/personalandhouseholdfinances/incomeandwealth/adhocs/13102uksharesandprivatepensionwealthbyhouseholdincomegreatbritainjuly2010tojune2016andapril2014tomarch2018

ONS (2022) 'Family spending in the UK: April 2021 to March 2022'. URL: ons.gov.uk/peoplepopulationandcommunity/personalandhouseholdfinances/expenditure/bulletins/familyspendingintheuk/april2021tomarch2022

Otis Leder, R (2019) 'Customer loyalty programs: what are they? (With examples)'. Salesforce. URL: salesforce.com/blog/customer-loyalty-program-examples-tips

Polkes, A (2020) 'The state of brand loyalty 2021: global consumer survey'. Yotpo. URL: yotpo.com/blog/the-state-of-brand-loyalty-2021-global-consumer-survey

PYMNTS (2022) 'Relationship commerce: building long-term brand engagement'. URL: pymnts.com/study/relationship-commerce-brand-engagement-subscriptions-memberships-loyalty-programs

Reich, R (2023) 'Wealth & poverty'. URL: youtube.com/playlist?list=PLOLArO56vjuoeaIPzKQibBDbx2m_Rfsit

Reichheld, F (2001) 'Prescription for cutting costs'. Bain & Company. URL: media.bain.com/Images/BB_Prescription_cutting_costs.pdf

Remund, D L (2010) 'Financial literacy explicated: the case for a clearer definition in an increasingly complex economy'. *The Journal of Consumer Affairs* June 2010.

Repko, M (2022) 'Walmart kicks off exclusive sales event to try to win and retain Walmart+ members'. CNBC. URL: cnbc.com/2022/02/24/walmart-kicks-off-exclusive-sales-event-for-walmart-members.html

Ricci, S A G & Sautter, C M (2022) 'How retail investing improves corporate governance and benefits society'. University of Oxford Faculty of Law. URL: blogs.law.ox.ac.uk/oblb/blog-post/2022/09/how-retail-investing-improves-corporate-governance-and-benefits-society

Ross-Smith, M (2022) 'Loyalty programs need more control to fuel growth of airline industry valuations'. Travel Data Daily. URL: traveldatadaily.com/loyalty-programs-fuel-growth-of-airline-industry

Simply Wall Street (2024) 'Tesco ownership'. URL: simplywall.st/stocks/gb/consumer-retailing/bats-chixe-tscol/tesco-shares/ownership

Sturrock, D (2023) 'Wealth and welfare across generations'. Institute for Fiscal Studies. URL: ifs.org.uk/sites/default/files/2023-04/WP202315-Wealth-and-welfare-across-generations.pdf

Sweet, E, Nandi, A et al (2013) 'The high price of debt: household financial debt and its impact on mental and physical health'. *Social Science & Medicine* August 2013.

Tesco (2023) 'Annual report and financial statements 2023'. URL: tescoplc.com/media/u1wlq2qf/tesco-plc-annual-report-2023.pdf

Thaler, R H & Sunstein, C R (2008) *Nudge: Improving decisions about health, wealth, and happiness.* Yale University Press.

Thomas, M E (2021) 'Poverty in a world of mass impoverishment'. 99%. URL: 99-percent.org/poverty-in-a-world-of-mass-impoverishment

TIME (1956) 'Business: the new conservatism'. URL: content.time.com/time/subscriber/article/0,33009,867385-2,00.html

Van Rooij, M, Lusardi, A & Alessie, R (2011) 'Financial literacy and stock market participation'. *Journal of Financial Economics* 101(2).

Wollan, R, Davis, P et al (2017) 'Seeing beyond the illusion: it's time you invest more wisely'. Accenture. URL: accenture.com/content/dam/accenture/final/a-com-migration/pdf/pdf-43/accenture-strategy-gcpr-customer-loyalty.pdf

Sources for figures

1. epi.org/productivity-pay-gap (this and various other figures via Reich 2023)
2. statista.com/statistics/269959/employment-in-the-united-states
3. statista.com/statistics/281992/employment-rate-in-the-united-kingdom

4. statista.com/statistics/263591/gross-domestic-product-gdp-of-the-united-states
5. statista.com/statistics/263590/gross-domestic-product-gdp-of-the-united-kingdom
6. nytimes.com/2020/08/18/business/stock-market-record.html
7. en.wikipedia.org/wiki/File:FTSE_100_index_chart_since_1984.png
8. motherjones.com/politics/2022/05/private-equity-buyout-kkr-houdaille
9. statista.com/statistics/1314034/private-equity-market-size-uk
10. statista.com/statistics/222130/annual-corporate-profits-in-the-us
11. economicshelp.org/blog/27428/economics/uk-company-profits
12. statista.com/chart/17679/real-wages-in-the-united-states
13. epi.org/publication/top-charts-of-2018-twelve-charts-that-show-how-policy-could-reduce-inequality-but-is-making-it-worse-instead
14. mainlymacro.blogspot.com/2022/06/why-has-uk-real-wage-growth-been-so-low.html
15. finance.yahoo.com/news/the-richest-1-own-50-of-stocks-held-by-american-households-150758595.html
16. nytimes.com/2021/01/26/upshot/stocks-pandemic-inequality.html
17. ons.gov.uk/economy/investmentspensionsandtrusts/bulletins/owner-shipofukquotedshares/2020
18. ons.gov.uk/economy/investmentspensionsandtrusts/bulletins/owner-shipofukquotedshares/2020
19. coursehero.com/file/plmdf11/B-Even-if-such-social-mobility-is-easi-er-I-sLll-wouldnt-accept-correspondingly
20. coursehero.com/file/plmdf11/B-Even-if-such-social-mobility-is-easi-er-I-sLll-wouldnt-accept-correspondingly
21. wir2022.wid.world/www-site/uploads/2021/12/WorldInequalityRe-port2022_Full_Report.pdf
22. wir2022.wid.world/methodology
23. positivemoney.org/2017/10/wealth-inequality
24. janushenderson.com/en-us/advisor/press-releases/global-share-buy-backs-surge-to-a-record-1-31-trillion-almost-equalling-dividends
25. Medina et al 2021
26. web-assets.bcg.com/76/eb/23e0e899414ba718c372e481072f/bcg-loyal-ty-programs-need-next-generation-june-2023.pdf
27. web-assets.bcg.com/76/eb/23e0e899414ba718c372e481072f/bcg-loyal-ty-programs-need-next-generation-june-2023.pdf
28. nytimes.com/2018/11/25/opinion/monopolies-in-the-us.html
29. indexes.morningstar.com/indexes/details/morningstar-wide-moat-focus-FSUSA07Z10

Acknowledgements

This book has taken many hours of thought and work. Heartfelt and profound thanks are therefore due to my family, who have been resolutely at my side throughout.

First, and most prominently, to my wife, Somita, and my children, Ayush and Aarav. Thank you for your unwavering support through my various adventures. I appreciate how you've tolerated a distant husband and dad whose brain has been engaged with saving capitalism rather than pressing concerns closer to home. Thank you!

Next, to my parents – my mother, Jharna, and my late dad, Bibhuti. Thank you for giving me the gift of education and for always encouraging and supporting me to think big.

Finally, thanks go to my brother, Bidesh Sarkar CBE, for always being a role model and source of support and guidance whenever needed.

EU Safety Representative: euComply OÜ Pärnu mnt 139b-14 11317 Tallinn
Estonia hello@eucompliancepartner.com +33 756 90241

www.ingramcontent.com/pod-product-compliance
Lightning Source LLC
Chambersburg PA
CBHW042122190326
41519CB00031B/7583